I AM GOLD DUST
(AND YOU ARE TOO)

To Sam —
Your courage, strength,
and grit have inspired me
countless times, inside & outside
the gym! I am so grateful
to have you in my life.
Thank you for helping
this dream of writing
a book become
a reality!
♡ S

I AM GOLD DUST (AND YOU ARE TOO)

MINDFULNESS AND AUTHENTICITY IN THE WORKPLACE

STEPHANIE VANZYTVELD

NEW DEGREE PRESS

I AM GOLD DUST (AND YOU ARE TOO)
Mindfulness and Authenticity in the Workplace

ISBN   978-1-64137-574-0 *Paperback*
          978-1-64137-575-7 *Kindle Ebook*
          978-1-64137-576-4 *Ebook*

Dedicated to my grandma, Christine VanZytveld,
and the memory of three people who helped my
gold dust shine its brightest:
Edna Seamons, Mary Wilhite, and Levi Felix

CONTENTS

I Am Gold Dust (and You Are Too):
Mindfulness and Authenticity in the Workplace

BY STEPHANIE VANZYTVELD

ACKNOWLEDGMENTS

I am grateful for the continuing support of Sally Hewitt, who lovingly waded through multiple drafts, helping me transform my passionate ramblings into cogent prose. Her keen eye and compassionate heart allowed me to temporarily take my ego offline and let another human being in—so I could convey the truth without dying of exposure.

I would like to thank Elissa Graeser, my developmental editor, who gently guided me through the terrifying process of showing my pages to another human being. Trusting her to help me sort through whatever tumbled out during those early excavations undoubtedly made this book better.

I am grateful for Eric Koester's vision, enthusiasm, and limitless energy. I am also grateful for Brian Bies, whose positivity (and love of Taylor Swift) convinced me it was safe to venture further out on the limb. Thank you to the teams at Creator Institute and New Degree Press, specifically Heather Gomez and Bailee Noelle.

I would like to thank Rachelle Sartini Garner for being the creative midwife for my Gold Dust & Co. vision back in 2015. She is also the brilliant calligrapher who designed the original Gold Dust logo and branding.

I am grateful for the love and support of my mom and dad, as well as my sister Jillian. She may be seven years younger, but has never hesitated to step into the role of Big Sister when needed.

I would like to thank Elizabeth Birnkrant, Mackie Berman, Ellen O'Rourke, and Amanda Nyren for their unconditional love and encouragement.

From the bottom of my heart, thank you to everyone at Camp Grounded and Spark for helping me to reconnect with my authentic Gold Dust self.

Without the generosity of the individuals who funded my pre-sale campaign, this book would not exist:

Alyssa Baum; Amanda Nyren; Amy Kozlowski; Andrew White; Annie Darby; Ashley Slover; Ben Raczka; Bill Hamilton; Bob Callahan; Bonnie Johnson; Bryan Hocker; Chas Wiederhold; Crystal Raygoza; Dan Polshaw; Dana Olthouse; Daniel and Joseph Goebel; Darcie Trier; David Sutor; Deidre Honig; Donovan James; Ehiman Uwidia; Elizabeth Birnkrant; Eric Koester; Erin DeVaney; Erin Doyle; Fred Jeske; Grace Geremias; Grace Kim; Holly Blukis; Howard J. Horwitz; Igor Melnik; Jennica Owens; Jennifer Heffernan; Jessica Magnatta; Jill Dreyer; Jill Wagar; Jill Wester; Jillian VanZytveld; John E. Nieuwenhuis; John

Taylor; Jutta Keenan; Karen Chouinard; Karishma Parekh; Kathy Ann Cook; Kelly O'Brien; Kelly Perez; Kimberly Lin; Kristen DeAngelis; Kristen Johnstone; Kristin Crane Harper; Lani Ashton Larkin; Laura Meierkort; Lauren Cali; Lauren Sammis; Leanne J. Gurley; Leslye Swigert; Lily Schmall; Luigi Mazzel; Lyndsey Kantarski; Mackie Berman; Maggie Meiners; Mandy Kass; Maritza Barajas; Mary Huskey; Mary Ortiz; Matt Tobel; Meghan Reid; Nicole Bird; Pamela Klier-Weidner; Pedro Guerrero; Rebecca Matthews; Rebecca VanZytveld; Ryan Wynia; Sally Hewitt; Sam Zacks; Samantha Gray; Sara Hohnstein; Sara Islas; Sara Lloyd; Scott Schieber; Sheila Brophy; Stephanie Janulis; Suchit Shah; Ted Wright; Thomas DiPrima; Urooj Malik

INTRODUCTION

UNEARTHING GOLD DUST

Several years ago, I took a leap and registered for a digital detox camp—where adults trade in their technology and real-world identities for a long weekend at summer camp in the redwoods of Northern California.

At camp, only a few rules apply, but they're strictly enforced:

- No technology
- No work talk (or "W" talk, to avoid using the word entirely)
- No real names

By the time camp rolled around, my fraying-at-the-edges, anxiety-ridden, type-A self couldn't seem to locate the desire that had pushed me to register in the first place. Still, I had settled the most important dilemma: My nickname would be Gold Dust—an homage to my ego ideal, Stevie Nicks.

When I emerged from my long weekend in the redwoods, I instinctively knew that Gold Dust was not just a character to be packed away with my sleeping bag. Gold Dust represented my authentic self—who I actually am at my core.

The titles, clothes, and props that surround me in my daily life as "Stephanie VanZytveld" are my costume. I'm a spiritual being having an experience on the material plane. While I love comfort as much as the next girl, I don't want to miss out on the real adventure of this lifetime because I was holed up in the existential gift shop, stocking up on tchotchkes.

If we strip away all the masks and labels that are part of living in a material world, I believe each of us has an inner compass. We can choose to follow it or ignore it. Every moment presents a new opportunity to discern where it's pointing and decide whether or not to head in that direction. I love sacred spaces like Camp Grounded, where I have the opportunity to be myself around like-minded people. However, my real work is to show up as Gold Dust in my daily life—the one that includes technology, the titles, and my real name. This is humbling, uncomfortable, and messy work; yet the alternative is not a life I want to live.

I know I'm not the only person trying to live an authentic life in a world that isn't always receptive to it. The workplace has been the most challenging arena in which to practice vulnerability. I relied on my self-defense mechanisms to keep me safe in the corporate world, but as time went on, the cost of pretending to be someone I'm not exacted a large toll. Until one day, when it stopped working entirely.

My virtue did not lead me to break this dysfunctional chain. I did not gladly turn and face the demons that generations before me had been running from. If I could still get away with numbing the pain, I would.

Even though I excelled at concealing them, the cracks were beginning to show. By the time I graduated high school, my bulimia and anxiety were already in full swing. Determined to be the first person in my family to attend college, I started at Calvin College, a Christian liberal arts school nearby. I wanted to leave after the first year, but allowed myself to be talked into returning. By the end of the second year, I'd withdrawn from half of my classes and barely made it out of the remaining two before dropping out entirely.

It would take another decade, six years of which would be spent in a failed marriage, but the darkness that consumed me, that I had kept so well-hidden, would eventually surface—despite my best attempts to drown it in alcohol, relationships, and body obsession. Then I'd basically have to wrestle with my own demons or risk passing them on inadvertently to the next generation, just like my mother did with me, and her mother with her, and so on.

Yet, my mother was the only one who had the courage to confront me about my alcoholism. While we sat waiting for the Amtrak train to pull into the station and bring me back to Chicago, she quietly looked over and said,

"You might want to do something about your drinking."

For her to risk my wrath, something inside me knew enough to listen.

My job title, my bank account, and my "I've-got-this" persona kept my ego so inflated; I'm amazed I could even hear her whispered suggestion behind my heavily-fortified walls. But the arrow went surprisingly deep—it made its way through the solitary crack in my armor. It was grace, not virtue, that compelled me to reach out for help. I'm grateful for the willingness I had in that moment to reach out for help. I'm equally grateful for the willingness to continue doing what I need to do, one day at a time, to heal.

Staying sober, both physically and emotionally, dramatically altered my daily life. I packed my schedule with activities to preoccupy myself and avoid the chance I'd have a moment to think and (heaven forbid!) feel what I'd been drinking to avoid.

Thanks to the emotional and physical exhaustion of living life without my medicine (i.e., alcohol), any remaining time outside of work was spent sleeping, or curled up in the fetal position while my mind tormented me.

I lived by myself at the time, which freed me from having to keep up any pretense that my life hadn't completely unraveled. Allowing myself to fall apart in my sponsor's living room or in recovery meetings was one thing—but a majority of my waking hours (and most people's) needed to occur in a work environment. Navigating my personal life was challenging on its own, but the professional realm took this to a whole new level.

I'd sacrificed so much to build my career—I couldn't risk losing it. I spent my early twenties as a hairdresser. Even though I worked in high-end salons and had a flourishing clientele, I couldn't afford my health insurance premiums. In 2000 and the early aughts, affordable health care didn't dominate the national conversation the way it does today. I researched the issue and learned that forty-six million Americans were uninsured, just like me. Determined to do something about that, I decided to leave the salon world and return to finish my undergraduate degree.

It took five years to complete my undergraduate and graduate work, but I achieved my goal. In 2007, I graduated with high distinction and departmental honors in Women's Studies from the University of Michigan. In 2010, I graduated with my Masters in Healthcare Administration from the School of Public Health at the University of Illinois at Chicago.

Laser-focused on climbing the corporate ladder as fast as I could, I had decided at the beginning of graduate school that I wanted to complete an administrative fellowship once I graduated. Similar to a fellowship for a medical or surgical specialty, an administrative fellowship is a one- to two-year program that further develops the fellow's knowledge base and experience by exposing them to people and projects they otherwise wouldn't encounter until much later in their career.

I achieved that goal as well, and accepted a fellowship at the University of Illinois Hospital & Health Sciences System. As one of two fellows that year, my colleague and I worked in the hospital's C-suite and were privy to all manner of enterprise politics and projects. The intense pressure and political skirmishes provided frequent opportunities for me to thrive under pressure. We were only halfway through our fellowships when both of us accepted full-time positions there.

Even though I was successful navigating the professional landscape, it felt like a war zone. As the knot in my chest continued to tighten throughout the day, I would remind myself that once the day was over, a drink would give me some relief. (Just watching the bottle of gin make its way down the conveyor belt to the cashier would begin to loosen that knot.) A combat soldier has weapons for offense and armor for defense. Alcohol was a significant part of my defensive strategy.

With alcohol no longer an option, my security blanket had been ripped away. With limited proficiency in my new coping mechanisms, my work life suddenly felt like I'd been dropped into hostile territory completely defenseless.

Fast forward eight years later: I'm not just surviving—I'm thriving.

EMOTIONS IN THE WORKPLACE

I began learning to stuff my emotions inside in grade school, but the indoctrination that women were "too emotional" started long before. I've been combatting the liabilities woven into my two X chromosomes since before I knew what a period was.

Born in 1980, I am on the cusp of Gen X and Millennials, a micro generation referred to as a Xennial. I grew up with an analog childhood and a digital adolescence. While not every child of the

80s was raised with these views, plenty of us were—especially those in areas where conservative evangelical values ran deep. I learned that, as a female, my sensitive, emotional nature precluded me from most leadership roles within the church. Even if I did achieve a leadership position in the corporate world, I'd risk being labeled a Feminazi by Rush Limbaugh or one of his fans. Plus, it would make it harder for me to attract a man.

Over the past twenty years, I've watched the pendulum swing back and forth. Old mindsets begin to crumble and new ones replace them. If I could say anything to my ten-year-old self, it would be to view what someone says and does as a sample size of one. Just because one man calls you an ugly name, doesn't mean that he speaks for all men. Also, cruelty is not gendered: hurt people hurt people, regardless of the pronouns they prefer.

During my postgraduate fellowship, I received a piece of wisdom from a director at the hospital where my peer and I worked. After a particularly heated meeting involving a number of executives, we sat on a bench in the courtyard, staring off at the ivy curling up the brick façade, in between sips of too-hot institutional coffee. Having just watched her run the emotional gauntlet without so much as breaking a sweat, I mentioned something about my fear of being perceived as too emotional.

She stopped me and explained,

"Men get emotional in the workplace all the time! Because their outbursts usually involve feelings of impatience, anger, or rage, those feelings are considered 'normal.'"

Once she pointed it out, I couldn't unsee it: Of the countless times I'd been screamed at in the workplace, the overwhelming majority happened opposite a man, often red in the face, with a vein popping or a finger pointing. The "heated discussion" may have included swearing, shoving papers, or throwing things. Or not. Rage is plenty potent when no energy is siphoned off to supporting acts. By that point I had three decades' worth of men seemingly incapable of making their point without a combination of volume or violence, and yet *I* was concerned about appearing too emotional?!

EMOTIONAL REGULATION

By the time I reached corporate America, I had adopted the same code of silence that keeps dysfunctional family systems intact: "Don't think. Don't talk. Don't feel." This coping mechanism, though flawed, is one way to avoid setting off any reactionary power brokers. I had nearly perfected the art of walking on eggshells, and I had an uncanny ability to intuit a manager's needs before he or she asked. These are the same behaviors that trap codependent people in dysfunctional relationships—yet they earned me accolades at work.

Despite what anyone says, humans can't check their emotional selves at the door and put them on again once the workday is over. Unless we are aware of the emotional weather patterns occurring in the background, and capable of recognizing when our emotions are overriding our control center, we are at the mercy of the part of our brain that is more reptilian in nature—the amygdala which handles the body's "fight, flight, or freeze" response. In his book,

Emotional Intelligence: Why It Can Matter More Than IQ,
Daniel Goleman labels extreme reactions to stress as an
amygdala hijack.[1]

HUMAN BEHAVIOR: 30 PERCENT LOGIC, 70 PERCENT EMOTION

We consider ourselves rational beings, but the lion's share of
decision-making is ruled by emotion. The field of behavioral
economics studies the patterns and predictability inherent
in human decision making. The general assumption held by
behavioral economists is that 30 percent of human behavior can be explained via logic, but 70 percent is based on
emotion.[2]

If humans were 100 percent logical in their decision-making, indices like GDP (Gross Domestic Product), household
income, and unemployment rates, would be good predic-
tors of human decision making. [3] However, with logic only
accounting for 30 percent of human decision-making, the
need for additional indicator types is clear. [4] Measures of
well-being, like the following Gallup study, provide insight
into the emotional component influencing the remaining 70
percent of human decision-making. [5]

---

1   "Amygdala Hijack: When Emotion Takes Over," Nancy Moyer, MD,
    Healthline.com, April 22, 2019, Accessed on January 25, 2020.
2   Jim Clifton, "What Happiness Today Tells Us About the World Tomor-
    row," Gallup.com, Accessed on September 27, 2019.
3   Jim Clifton, "What Happiness Today Tells Us About the World Tomor-
    row," Gallup.com, Accessed on September 27, 2019.
4   Ibid.
5   Ibid.

For readers within the US, an additional cause for concern exists: We don't acknowledge the role emotions play in our decision-making, and as a country, our overall emotional well-being is tanking. [6]

Gallup's global survey entitled "What Happiness Today Can Tell Us About the World Tomorrow" measures emotional state by country and its change overtime. [7]

Over the past decade, the percentage of people thriving in the US has dropped by 10 percent: 56 percent compared to 66 percent in 2007. [8]

The protracted economic downturn following the crash in 2007 is a contributing factor; however, it's important to note that equating the reduction in thriving to economic pressures is still only speaking to the 30 percent of rational decision-making. [9]

The US is one of eight countries experiencing the largest reduction in those considered "thriving," a list that includes New Zealand, India, and Greece. [10]

Research by George Ward, of the London School of Economics, maintains that measures of well-being (like this Gallup study) are better indicators of election outcomes because of

6   Ibid.
7   Ibid.
8   Jim Clifton, "What Happiness Today Tells Us About the World Tomorrow," Gallup.com, Accessed on September 27, 2019.
9   Ibid.
10 Ibid.

the influence feelings have on an individual's voting decisions. [11] In the Brexit decision, and in the divisive 2016
US election, the decline in percentage of those considered
thriving in the years leading up to both results was a better
predictor than average household income. [12]

WORKPLACE ENGAGEMENT IS ALSO FLAGGING

A majority of people are unsatisfied with their work lives as
well. Gallup has studied employee engagement—defined as
an employee being "involved in, enthusiastic about and committed to their work and workplace"—since 2000. [13] Today,
only 15 percent of employees are engaged worldwide. [14] US
worker engagement is slightly better, at 30 percent. [15] Over
the past 15 years, these numbers have remained essentially
the same, indicating that current approaches to improving
engagement are ineffective, which negatively impacts produc-
tivity and ultimately the organization's well-being. [16]

ANSWERS? ANYBODY?

I am beyond disillusioned with leadership books. Honestly, even
the proliferation of the TedTalk look and feel is starting to get on

---

11   Ibid.

12   Jim Clifton, "What Happiness Today Tells Us About the World Tomor-
     row," Gallup.com, Accessed on September 27, 2019.

13   Annamarie Mann and Jim Harter, "The Worldwide Employee Engage-
     ment Crisis," Gallup.com, Accessed on September 28, 2019.

14   Jim Clifton, "The World's Broken Workplace," Gallup.com. Accessed on
     September 28, 2019.

15   Ibid.

16   Annamarie Mann and Jim Harter, "The Worldwide Employee Engage-
     ment Crisis," Gallup.com, Accessed on September 28, 2019.

my nerves. A lot of great stuff exists out there, but I still feel like there's an elephant in the room. (Multiple elephants, actually.) Our world is changing so fast, it's hard to find the motivation for self-improvement with all the big issues looming large, like:

- The climate crisis that threatens our world
- Power structures that continue to disadvantage people based on the intersection of their identities, such as race, gender, class, sexuality, etc.
- Threats to our democracy, both foreign and domestic
- Staggering income inequality
- Astronomical student loan debt

Note: The irony that I'm writing a book advocating personal changes is not lost on me, especially when I don't have the solutions to all these big, scary things either.

Between genuine threats to our way of life and the continuing evidence that much of what conventional wisdom has taught us was wrong—the housing bubble, bank bailouts, the middle class shouldering the highest tax rate of any income bracket—forgive me if I'm not interested in your advice on how to optimize my LinkedIn profile.

Yet, today I work in the most conservative corporate environment I've ever worked in, and I'm able to show up as myself. This book contains the guidance I so desperately sought, but never found, in countless brown-bag presentations and breakout sessions.

I've found it really is true that each of us has the innate ability to get where we're going, but we don't talk about it much because:

- We don't know/trust/use it ourselves
- Topics involving mystery can be uncomfortable to discuss, and are often dismissed as too "woo-woo" or fringe
- Then you don't need the latest product/service/quick fix

COMMON TERMS AND HOW I USE THEM

This book covers topics that are squishy enough in nature. To bring some clarity to the discussion, here are common terms I'll be using, and how I define them.

The term **ego** can be used in multiple ways. I think of it as the near-continuous chatter in my brain, providing colorful commentary (both positive and negative) as I move throughout the world. In fact, this internal narration is actually one of the numerous tactics my ego uses to regulate my self-esteem, helping me feel in control of my surroundings (that I actually have no control over, whatsoever).

If pressed to select a more scientific definition, my definition of ego most closely aligns to the concept of unchecked egotism and its more desirable counterpart, the quiet ego, defined by Jack J. Bauer and Heidi A. Wayment: "the quiet ego and quieting the ego...connote the individual who routinely transcends egotism as well as the need to turn down a few notches the booming volume of egotism, on both individual and cultural levels." [17]

---

17 Jack J. Bauer & Heidi A. Wayment, "The psychology of the quiet ego" in *Decade of Behavior. Transcending Self-Interest: Psychological Explorations of the Quiet Ego,* eds. H. A. Wayment & J. J. Bauer, (Washington, D.C.: American Psychological Association, 2008), 7–19.

Mindfulness is the ability to notice thought patterns and redirect my attention to those that support the best version of myself. Mindfulness practices help me quiet the ego.

Mindlessness is the opposite of mindfulness: having no distinction between my thoughts and my reality. In a mindless state, I'm going through life on autopilot, with my unobserved brain providing the algorithm, often in a state of unchecked egotism.

Authenticity is acting from my true self regardless of the setting. By setting appropriate and flexible boundaries, I am still able to choose how little or how much of my **authentic self** (or **best self**) I share in a given setting, depending on the situation and the level of trust I have with the person, people, or institution concerned. I rely on my **inner compass** (my **intuition**) to guide the location and rigidity of those boundaries, which may be revised over time to suit a relationship's particular needs. In its simplest form, authenticity is action taken in the material world on behalf of love.

QUIETING THE EGO HAS A PARADOXICAL EFFECT ON THE SELF

In their book, *Transcending Self-Interest: Psychological Explorations of the Quiet Ego,* Heidi A. Wayment, PhD, and Jack J. Bauer, PhD, explore psychology's definition of the self. [18] Rather than critique the negative impacts of our increasingly

---

18 Heidi A. Wayment, PhD, and Jack J. Bauer, PhD., eds. *Transcending Self-Interest: Psychological Explorations of the Quiet Ego*, Washington D.C.: American Psychological Association, 2008.

self-obsessed society, the editors' compilation outlines two useful paths toward quieting the ego:

- Caring for oneself in order to care for others
- Developing compassionate self-awareness and interdependence with others [19]

Writing for *Scientific American,* Dr. Scott Barry Kaufman, Psychologist at Columbia University, builds on the Quiet Ego research pioneered by Wayment and her colleagues. Quieting the ego has a paradoxical effect: Instead of diminishing the self, quieting the ego allows one's authentic self to shine more brightly. [20]

TRIALS, TRIBULATIONS, AND LESSONS LEARNED

I'm writing this because I've experienced a number of the career landmines people don't talk about on graduation day, and that's when I definitely needed some encouragement—and some advice.

- I've been through a significant career change—from a hairdresser to a healthcare management consultant—and know what it's like to go back to finish your undergraduate degree years after dropping out.
- I went to graduate school and competed for administrative fellowships, then had to earn my stripes all over again in a different field.
- I've weathered good bosses, heinous bosses, and everyone in between.

---

19 Ibid.
20 Scott Barry Kaufman, Ph.D., "The Pressing Need for Everyone to Quiet Their Egos," *Scientific American*, May 21, 2018, Accessed on December 21, 2019.

- I've learned how to speak truth to power, advocate for myself, and display courage even when the people above me on the organizational chart didn't model that behavior.
- In 2018, I arranged my own sabbatical and spent thirteen weeks surfing around the coast of South Africa and Mozambique.
- Even when reality is unpleasant or uncomfortable, ($100K+ in student loan debt, anyone?) I continue to find ways to build the life I want, while loving the one I already have.

Most importantly, I've learned to be my authentic self in the workplace—and hold space for other people who aren't comfortable enough in their own skin to do so...yet. One of the best rewards of doing this work is watching the ripple effect it has on everyone in your life: When I'm around someone who's being true to their authentic self, I can feel it in my body, and I'm inspired to do the same.

THE CASE FOR A LITTLE REMYSTIFICATION

"Intuition does not denote something contrary to reason, but something outside of the province of reason."

—C.G. JUNG [21]

---

21 Carl G. Jung, qtd. in Quotable Quote, Goodreads (website), Accessed on December 20, 2019.

I am well aware of the silent pact we uphold that keeps us respectable business folk from talking about matters that deal with the heart, emotion, or (gasp!) faith. I'll delve further into this issue in the upcoming chapters. For now, though, I'd like to offer you the idea that cutting off parts of our humanity (i.e., anything that doesn't fit neatly into the logical, rational, explainable, measurable box) IS NOT WORKING.

By not making space for our shared humanity, the unaddressed emotions of human suffering are already running the show in countless lives—those of our colleagues, neighbors, and friends. We just can't see them, or hear them, because we've collectively agreed that they're not acceptable topics of conversation.

I'm not advocating we swing the pendulum wildly in the direction of unchecked emotion either!

Our current approach appears to advocate pulling oneself up by one's bootstraps, with self-medicating the best one can as a close second. By waiting for a particular coping mechanism(s) to become sanitized enough for public consumption (i.e., when my suffering is reduced to a data point on a population's prevalence of alcohol dependence, obesity, clinical depression, etc.,) we will continue this madness of talking about uncomfortable subjects only after they've reached levels high enough to trigger public health warnings.

I'm not advocating that the workplace become a therapeutic environment, or that managers become de facto social workers, or anything of the sort. My only request is that if you experience any personal discomfort while reading the ideas presented here that you stay with them just a little longer than you might have, had I not asked. In sticking with that discomfort just a tiny bit longer than we otherwise might have, we're teaching our whole selves (our brains and our hearts) to remain flexible. That ability to change ourselves and make more space for other people with different views, produces a ripple effect that not only helps you acknowledge the brilliance of your own authentic self, but recognize it in others as well.

IT'S NOT EITHER/OR, IT'S BOTH/AND

Career-related guidance seems to be focused on the head, with any nod to the heart as an afterthought at best. While leadership books do a better job addressing our soft skills, they do so from a clinical, sanitized lens. This means the heart gets talked about in a way that still leaves the reader comfortably in their own head. When I'm in my head theorizing, I'm not out on the field honing my skills. This allows me to pat myself on the back for having spent time thinking about making a change, without any of the discomfort that goes along with actually changing.

PAYING IT FORWARD

Recently, I volunteered to help review recent grad's resumes at a work event for my corporate job. I've shied away from anything networking related for the past few years (unless it's 100 percent mandatory) because I hate small talk, phoniness, and ego—and I can't seem to go to these events without feeling like that's all they are. But this event was being held for students who were first generation college grads, and as the first person in my family to graduate from college, I felt a special pull to pay it forward. I followed my impulse, signed up, and showed up.

The keynote speaker delivered some pragmatic and thoughtful advice, but secretly, I wished it was me at that lectern because I had so much to share. Then the panel on career advice began. It took all the strength I had to keep from running up there, grabbing the mic away from one of the panelists, and directing them to take a seat in the audience. Grateful for my improved impulse control (and slightly alarmed by the intensity of my emotional response) I realized that I *did* have something to say. It's not just ego-based nonsense either; it's actually hard won and valuable experience that is applicable and available to everyone.

HEY! YEAH, YOU!

Whether you're a new grad, disillusioned with your current career and considering a change, or seeking specifics about what it looks like to be an authentic person in an office environment versus theory—this book is for you. If you're not sure what you're looking for...well, this book might be for you too.

Drawing from others' stories as well as my own, in addition to findings from experts in the field, we'll explore:

- Why "following your bliss" is actually sage advice
- Specific mindfulness practices to help you turn down your ego's volume knob
- Following your Inner Compass to direct your day-to-day activities, which ultimately directs your career

- Guidance on taming your Inner Critic
- How to differentiate between your ego and your authentic self

In the following pages you'll learn that there's no "there" to achieve or find—which means relief is much closer than you think. You'll discover superpowers you had no idea you possessed (seriously). You'll begin working with the tools that will allow you to walk through the world being comfortable in your own skin.

Using mindfulness practices to connect with my authentic self continues to transform all aspects of my life. Perhaps the best part of this work is that you already have everything you need—so let's get started!

XO,

gold dust

PART 1

UNEARTHING GOLD DUST

CHAPTER 1

WHEN THE OLD WAY
QUIT WORKING

———

By the age of eleven, I had already wanted to be a number of things, including a hair stylist, a TV news anchor (I worshiped *Murphy Brown*), an author, an interior designer (Mom usually let me stay up to watch *Designing Women*), and a stock trader. I remember seeing a movie that depicted chaos on a trading floor, and instinctively knew I'd be good working in that kind of an environment.

I knew I'd be good at anything then.

The world was my oyster and whatever I set my mind to do, I would achieve. But as is the case with most adolescent girls, I'd soon learn that vocalizing such beliefs was frowned upon, and that my intelligence should be kept hidden.

Primarily so as not to intimidate the boys.

THE MAPS WE'RE HANDED

When my parents graduated high school in 1970, there were plenty of job options that didn't require a four-year degree. Both of them achieved success by relying on their intelligence, natural curiosity, and a solid work ethic.

My father, Steve, was a truck driver for Steelcase, the high-end office furniture manufacturer headquartered in Grand Rapids, Michigan. A stark contrast to the stereotypical trucker image, Steelcase's fleet of drivers adhered to strict rules governing uniforms and conduct.

My father's impeccable work ethic landed him the coveted job of driving one of Steelcase's two show trucks. In addition to hauling loads of office furniture to buyers around the country, these well-appointed semitrucks were frequently on display at design shows and promotional events. This was the late 80s/early 90s, long before reality shows like MTV's *Pimp My Ride* popularized customized vehicles. My father's truck boasted amenities like a waterbed, TV, and VCR, and a sink with running water, which were all quite novel at the time.

The perks of driving the show truck were balanced out by the additional responsibilities of maintaining the vehicle: countless evenings and days off spent detailing the interior and exterior of the massive truck, including polishing the tractor and trailer's chrome wheels by hand. These were often used to illustrate the value of hard work, and the sacrifices required to make it to the "elite" ranks of the particular field to which one belonged.

My mother, Becky, began working as an operator at the telephone company and eventually moved into telephone installation. As one of the first female telephone installers in Grand Rapids, she took pride in climbing the telephone poles using her boots, looking down on the installers who opted to climb a ladder instead. She often told stories from her time working for the phone company. Most tales seemed to be triggered by geographic location. If we passed by a building where she'd done some installation work, she'd point it out and recall an anecdote that happened there. My mom is an intelligent and detail-oriented woman. Even her stories involving pranks on fellow co-workers seemed like the sort of hijinks management let slide because of her team's reputation for stellar performance.

My mom had no patience for mistakes due to carelessness. After a few too many red marks on my first-grade math assignments, she began hounding me to "check my work." Instead of reaping the rewards of finishing an assignment early—like getting to head outside for recess before my class-mates, or just stare off into space while the other kids finished—she instructed me to review each math problem, one by one, to make sure I hadn't made any mistakes. At first, I complied, because I knew she'd ask me if I had checked my work. After several recesses of not getting outside fast enough to secure one of the "good" swings, my quality control methods went out the window. I'd scan the page to make sure that I hadn't left any blanks and hope for the best.

Though the versions I heard were softened by memory, my mom's stories of working outside in the cold haunted me. Growing up in the Midwest, I only liked spending recess outside a few months out of the year. I couldn't imagine having to be out in the elements as part of my job. It's not that my mom was campaigning for me to follow in her footsteps either—my parents both viewed a college education as my best chance at a flexible and satisfying career, and made it clear that my job was to prioritize my education to get my brain to take me as far as it could.

* * *

What we didn't know about my brain then (but we do now) is this: The same machine we were counting on to deliver me scholarship money was also prone to the histories of mental illness and untreated addiction running down both sides of my family tree.

* * *

I believe my parents knew on some level that the world was changing and that hard work and scrappiness wouldn't be sufficient to provide for my future. Conversely, I actually think all of us (myself included) put too much faith in the power of a college degree. Even graduating with high distinction and departmental honors from the University of Michigan was not the golden ticket we'd assumed it would be. Instead, it seemed to be no more than table stakes.

TO MY FAMILY

My parents both exemplified pluck and sacrifice when it came to raising me, and my sister, Jillian, born seven years and ten days later. We didn't know then what we know now about generational trauma, and the fact that unresolved emotional wounds work their way through a family tree (much in the same way a gene mutation might) until they're exposed, addressed, and healed.

In writing this, I struggle to balance my truth (as humans, to tell a story is to spin it in some fashion) with respect for my immediate and extended family members. I have learned over time to embrace the freedom and healing that comes with making the unspeakable, speakable. Just because I am accustomed to the light and thrive here, doesn't mean that others connected to me are ready and willing for that level of exposure.

I don't want to cause any additional harm in the service of healing my wounds. Conversely, I don't feel it's right for me to withhold my experience and hope from someone who needs it, especially if that fear is just perpetuating the same dysfunctional systems that are keeping us trapped. This is one of many examples where quieting my ego allows me to let my inner compass tell me where the balance between the two lies.

Here are some of the myriad ways in which my perspective on this matter gives me an unfair advantage:

- Hindsight being 20/20
- A generation of progress in the field of behavioral medicine, in both diagnosis of, and treatment for, mental illnesses
- Decreased stigma around mental illness
- Early exposure to cognitive behavioral therapy, and financial support for those weekly sessions when I couldn't afford health insurance (even if I had been able to afford

coverage, visits to mental health care providers weren't covered to the same extent because mental health parity laws didn't exist at the time)

- A hyperconnected world, where information is but a mere Google search away
- A culture so obsessed with self-documentation that my writing about my own endless fascination with how my mind both works—and works against me—seems quaint by comparison

Finally, I do not have children. I do not know what it is like to want the best for another human, and to pour copious amounts of time and energy into them, only to watch them self-destruct.

To my family, your love and support has brought me to a place where I have a wealth of resources at my disposal to face and feel the human shortcomings, found in any family tree, that perpetuate pain as long as they go unacknowledged and unaddressed. Shame is no one's birthright—that is a title only love can claim.

LINING UP THE DOMINOES

As a child, I began drafting maps of my future. By then, my map had several main destinations already on it, including: go to college, get married, have children, and live happily ever after. I'd flip through the giant J.C. Penny catalog and find pictures to represent my future life.

These amazing publications arrived once a year. The full-color pages contained pictures and descriptions of the entire department store's merchandise. I'd comb through them as though I were ordering up my future life, selecting who I wanted to be and the type of guy I wanted to marry. If I found someone cute, but was unimpressed with his Sansabelt slacks, I'd paste that guy's head on the body of someone who was dressed better.

Depending on what era of my life I was attempting to construct, I could find pictures of my wedding dress and dresses for my bridesmaids. If I was looking further into the future, I could find pictures of my kids and some furniture for our living room. Once I showed one of my collages to my uncle, an environmentalist and animal rights activist, who then lectured me about the dangers of overpopulation. (I'd picked a blonde woman wearing maternity clothes and had pasted two additional children in the picture.)

For my readers who grew up in the digital age, think of this exercise as an analog version of Pinterest. More than three decades later, we have a name for this—it's called a vision board. (Spoiler alert: I love those too.)

My answer to the question, "What do you want to be when you grow up?" changed depending on the day; however, I knew what kind of life I didn't want: the one I saw my parents living. My parents seemed to be constantly stressed. When my father wasn't on the road, he was sleeping or working on his side business, buying and selling custom truck parts. While at first my mother returned to work after having me, she then began working at home full-time when I turned one. Though she referred to herself as a stay-at-home mom, she was constantly answering the phone, fulfilling orders, dropping off shipments at UPS, and making local deliveries herself.

When I looked at examples of what I did want, the common denominator appeared to be a college education and the financial security it promised. With a successful career and financial stability now set as my ultimate goal, I reverse engineered my life plans to arrive at that end point. Life became a constant exercise in lining up the dominoes with precision—and then realigning them the second something unexpected occurred.

While my approach eventually backfired, I reverse engineered my life with a dogged persistence until that fateful day arrived.

REVERSE ENGINEERING "HAPPILY EVER AFTER"

With so much instability going on around me, I reached for the most stable-looking option I could imagine: Marrying my high school sweetheart, who had already spent two years at Calvin College, working his way toward seminary, and then a future as a minister. At eighteen, my plan was to head to Calvin too, and become an elementary school teacher. I knew numerous women who had followed this exact path—and for many of them, it worked. Nothing is wrong with that path, or any path, for that matter. Each of us is doing the best we can with the tools and information we have at hand.

I can't speak to anyone's motivation, nor could they to mine, but I suspect that this option worked for many of the women around me because they were being true to who they were and what they wanted.

One of the many reasons this path didn't work for me was because I designed it in response to fear. I wanted safety and security—I didn't care whether it lit me up inside or not. It made sense that, on days when my general anxiety had subsided, I found alternative paths more appealing. My fear-based selection didn't sit well with this suddenly more optimistic version of myself.

My parents gave me everything they had, but I had gone beyond the pale of their experience. Again, I don't have children, but that must be excruciating: To know that you're preparing them to take flight and go beyond the places you've seen and experienced—which also means that, if you're successful, you're readying them to go to places that you won't be able to help them navigate.

My parents couldn't equip me with tools they didn't have, and I'm not sure I would have taken advantage of those tools if they had been available. These appear to be lessons that can only be learned through experience. Had I not struggled to learn these lessons, I'd have no material for this book. And no need to search inward and become reacquainted with my authentic, Gold Dust self.

WHAT'S YOUR MAJOR?

Before my first semester even began, I broke up with my boyfriend. The world was turning out to be so much bigger than I had imagined, and I intuitively felt I deserved to explore it unencumbered.

Beyond all the new people I was meeting, new ideas were being introduced to me constantly. Rather than stay married to my previous career plans, I felt I owed it to myself to explore my options before settling on a major. In hindsight, these "leaps" from the safety of my planned path are so tame they're humorous. At the time, however, the stakes could not have felt higher. In the course of interviewing people for this book, I was grateful to learn I wasn't alone making such a monumental shift in early college life.

When I asked my friend, Ryan David Heywood—who I've only ever known as a professional actor, entrepreneur, and endurance athlete—I was shocked to learn his original life plan was essentially the same as my own.

Ryan grew up in Nebraska, and excelled in math and running. Impressed by the respect his track coach received from his teammates and himself, Ryan easily mapped out his future: He'd become a math teacher, coach the track team, and build a nice Nebraskan life.

Ryan explains, "That was as big as I could dream."

After high school graduation, he attended Doane University, a liberal arts college in Crete, Nebraska. The school not only offers guaranteed job placement for teachers it graduates each year—it also provides a warranty to the hiring institution. From the perspective of any eighteen-year-old heading out into the world, a scenario like this undercuts any condescending adult claiming that life offers no guarantees.

There was only one problem: Halfway through Ryan's sophomore year, he was having second thoughts. At this point, Doane required its students to declare a major. His stomach in knots, Ryan picked up the phone to call his father.

"Dad...," his voice hesitated.

"Yeah son?"

"I need to tell you something."

"Yeah?"

"I...I'm going to be an English major."

After a pause, Ryan's dad asked, "What are you going to do with an English major?"

"I don't know, Dad."

After hanging up the phone, Ryan returned to his theater friends, lamenting how his father had just rejected him. They nursed his wounds by driving around country roads and drinking beer.

Ryan recalls the remaining events of that evening with the same dramatic flair I'd applied to my own crises of faith during my late teens and early twenties.

Perhaps this is the only drawback of a lifetime of benefiting from straight, white privilege: We've got to supply our own drama to any bump in the road we can find because, the truth is, life has still dealt us a pretty nice hand.

Declaring a different major may not seem like a life-altering revelation, but there's no reason one can't wring his hands as though it were. I sure did.

ENACTING MY BEST LAID PLANS...
AND STILL HITTING BOTTOM

I started at Calvin College, but dropped out after my second year. It was difficult to pinpoint the source of my crippling anxiety and depression. The two main culprits appeared to be the growing student loan debt in the service of no identifiable career path and the long history of untreated mental illness running through my lineage. I dropped out, went to cosmetology school, and used my willingness to go the extra mile, along with a commitment to exceed my clients' expectations, to quickly build a successful career.

My anxiety and depression returned several years later, making it clear I needed professional help beyond my weekly cognitive behavioral therapy sessions. This was in the early 2000s, when I'd already aged off my parents' health insurance coverage. The cost to buy my own policy, especially one that would cover behavioral health benefits, was astronomical. I began to research the matter and realized that forty-six million other people were in the same predicament.

I'd already been toying with the idea of returning to school—the thrill of a massive undertaking stimulated my imagination, and helped transport me out of the real world any time I found it less-than-satisfying. I decided I was going to become a lawyer and fix the healthcare system.

But first, I'd have to finish my undergraduate degree.

Unfortunately, this meant going back to Calvin College and trying to salvage what I could from the final semester I spent there. (I'd withdrawn from several classes to avoid the F's I would have received had I stayed, but I failed to follow-up on the actual "withdrawing" part, so those W's had turned into F's anyway.)

I reached out to two of my former English professors, and both were kind enough to walk me through the steps I needed to take to get things moving in the right direction again. They wrote me letters of recommendation, which I included with my applications to institutions all over the country, determined to get into the best school that would have me. The University of Michigan was first to offer me acceptance, as did Columbia University in Manhattan, shortly afterward. It was 2005, and I was married at the time, so we decided to live apart while I went to Ann Arbor to finish my degree.

In 2007, I graduated with high distinction and departmental honors in Women's Studies. I'd been accepted to St. Louis University Law School, which had the top health law program at the time; but I was fairly certain that a Masters in Health-care Administration was more appropriate for the type of work I wanted to do, so I attended the University of Illinois at Chicago School of Public Health instead. I graduated with my MHA in 2010 and accepted a full-time position at the University of Illinois Hospital & Health Sciences System.

Whatever I lacked in innate ability, I made up for in person-ality, professionalism, and perseverance. I learned later that the ability to assimilate is a common trait among first-gen-eration college graduates. All my life I'd been observing the unspoken, unwritten rules that everyone else seemed to be aware of except me. Whether real or imagined, I never felt like I belonged—it was like I'd skipped class the day they handed out the handbook to life.

I might not have had the handbook, but I was determined to look like I did.

AN IMPECCABLE FAÇADE

I lived two lives: At work, I projected complete confidence. The minute I got home, I swapped out my J. Crew suit for a hoodie and sweatpants. I'd pour myself a gin and tonic and numb out until it was time for bed. At thirty-one, my life looked great on paper, but it was a sham.

Constantly spinning the plates and keeping up the impressive façade took a toll. My marriage was on the rocks, and couples counseling wasn't getting us anywhere. Even though I insisted I didn't have a problem, I couldn't wait until the workday was finished so I could have a drink. Or two. Or seven. By my logic, I couldn't possibly be an alcoholic if I was so successful in other areas. What I couldn't admit at the time was that I had no idea how I'd cope with the insanity of my job (and frankly, my life) without the promise of alcohol to numb away the pain at the end of each day.

In June of 2011, our divorce was final.

Seven weeks later, I got sober.

It's been eight years since then, and I've weathered all kinds of work situations without needing a drink: toxic bosses, sexual harassment, promotions, being recruited to a different sector of the industry, sudden layoffs, speaking truth to power, and plenty of others.

I've already mentioned two big issues—behavioral health and recovery from substance abuse—though this book is not meant to address either. I owe a debt I can never repay to behavioral health professionals (i.e., psychiatrists, therapists, etc.) and twelve-step recovery programs. *If you sense you may need professional help in either of those areas, I encourage you to seek it out.* Gratefully, the stigma associated with getting the help we need in these areas is decreasing, but I understand how scary it can be to reach out. Please do it anyway.

OUR MOST IMPORTANT WORK APPEARS TO BE AN INSIDE JOB

I spent the first half of my life thinking that the answers were outside of me—that if I just worked, tried, and studied hard enough, I'd eventually arrive at this place called "happiness."

From birth, we're surrounded by messages about how to navigate life. Parents, teachers, friends, advertisers, consciously or unconsciously contribute to the overall map we're making to guide us through this journey called life.

By the time I reached the monumental forks in the road (i.e., going to college, getting married, etc.), my maps contained input from numerous sources: prominent people in my life, general consensus from my community, as well as the constant stream of messaging from media and advertising. The data points ranged from specific, pointed advice to unspoken generalities and prevailing wisdom. A naturally curious person, with a strong defiant streak, I thought I'd thoroughly challenged all perspectives and formulated my own response.

And I had.

What I *hadn't* planned on was the need to reevaluate whether my original destination still made sense in light of the growth and change I'd experienced. As my understanding of people and the world evolves, so must my maps and my methodology for using them to navigate territory that's uncharted, at least by me.

Trusting inherited maps and stacking up dominoes eventually stopped working for me. Trying to manage every aspect of my life so that the outcomes matched my desires was impossible, exhausting, and fueled my penchant for self-destruction. I had to learn a whole new way to live life. And face some subjects I swore I'd never wrestle with again.

CHAPTER 2

ARE YOU THERE STEVIE? IT'S ME, STEPHANIE

———

"Religion is for people afraid of going to hell, spirituality is for people who've already been there."

—VINE DELORIA JR.[22]

FINDING RELIEF
(SOMEWHERE BESIDES A DRINK...OR A MAN)

"Now, you're going to hear them talk about God, but it's not what you think," Laurie cautioned.

My stomach dropped. Normally, I'd have put up more of a fight. At the very least, I would have submitted my intellectual case for the record. But I was too exhausted.

———

22 Deloria, Jr., Vine, Qtd. In "Vine Deloria, Jr.: Quotable Quotes," Goodreads (website), Accessed December 20, 2019.

"Just fake it 'til you make it," Laurie continued.

I ran my hand along the edge of the break room countertop. Someone had recently peeled back the Formica strip, exposing a new section of the particleboard underneath. Unlike the previous chunk, where the surface had been buffed down over time, these edges were raw. Just like me.

"Okay, so I'll see you at quarter to noon tomorrow, at the entrance closest to the Van Buren stop," I said.

I'd never been to the Board of Trade before. If I had to go to a twelve-step meeting, I figured I might as well go to the classy kind. Who knows? Maybe this was how I'd meet my next husband?

"Laurie...thank you," I said quietly.

"Don't mention it. See you tomorrow," Laurie replied.

When Laurie first told me she was in recovery, I likely had a horrified look on my face. Why would anyone disclose something as shameful as that?! Especially to someone who was only a work acquaintance?! Then again, Laurie was tall, blonde, and model thin—and she wore designer labels with aplomb.

Status seeking and vanity are two of my less-endearing traits, but they helped me find my way to a room of sober people. Since I was being superficial, it was a good thing Laurie looked like she had what I wanted or I may not have made it there.

Based on what I'd gathered from television, a twelve-step recovery meeting consisted of metal folding chairs,

Styrofoam cups of shitty coffee, and a bare light bulb or two, hanging from a ceiling. (This description would also fit the police station in any procedural crime show. I watched a lot of *Law & Order* marathons during my drinking career, so I may have conflated the two.)

Laurie was right—they did talk about God. And I was not a fan.

Too many horrible things had happened for there to be a God. Some of the worst people I knew considered themselves Christians.

I didn't believe in God, yet I was still terrified of spending eternity in hell. This double bind made me suicidal and suicide-proof. All the evidence seemed to indicate that I was on my own—that the recess mom who was supposed to be watching the playground never showed up for duty.

On the other hand, what if I jumped in front of a train only to learn that I was wrong? I'd spend eternity burning in hell, kicking myself for not having stuck it out to die of natural causes. While I generally don't advocate letting fear run one's life, in this instance the hellfire and damnation I'd absorbed as a child did keep me from venturing too far onto the blue line marking the L platform's edge.

YOU MEAN I'M NOT THE ONLY ONE?!

While I didn't meet my next husband at that recovery meeting, something miraculous *did* happen. And "miracle" is not a word I use lightly.

Everyone went around the room sharing their personal stories, and I felt at home for the first time in my life. I heard people putting words to feelings I thought were uniquely mine. Before that afternoon, I didn't feel like anyone would understand what it felt like to be in my skin. If they did, they'd understand that the negative side effects of my drinking were nothing compared to the torture of feeling life untempered. While the details varied, our stories were the same.

I heard people describe what it was like living with an obsessive mind, a hamster spinning on its wheel, hell-bent on getting the relief found in the next drink. My body clearly didn't process alcohol the way a non-drinker's body did: the minute alcohol got into my system, it was like Russian roulette. I might be able to stop after two or three drinks—I never had just one—or I might go into a blackout and wake up the next morning in a panic, with no idea how I'd gotten home. I'd swear I'd never drink again—*and really mean it this time!* By the next evening, I'd have rationalized some new reason why *this* time would be different.

As I sat in that meeting, I noticed an occasional wave of warmth and safety washing over me. My addled mind would quickly find something to obsess about and pull me back down into my usual state of despair and self-loathing. Every now and then, though, my shoulders would relax. I guess that foreign feeling was what others called "hope."

I decided to go to another meeting the next day. And the next. Women gave me their phone numbers, and I called a few of them. Some of the women I'd exchanged numbers with called me first. I was so grateful for the interruption that I picked up the phone before remembering how much

I hated talking to people. But these people didn't do small talk—which I appreciated. I could talk honestly about whatever was going on and not feel judged. While I was listening to them, I could feel my heart begin to soften, ever so slightly. Somehow, I'd made it through my first weekend without having a drink. I wasn't always warm and fuzzy about it, though—especially when this became an issue of needing to trust in a power greater than myself.

In the days after that first meeting, I kept doing what people suggested: a "90 in 90" (shorthand for ninety meetings in ninety days), getting the names and phone numbers of other sober women and calling them, even though I didn't yet feel like drinking. I kept hearing about the need to get a sponsor and "work the steps." I hadn't gotten to that yet, but I already sensed it was important. I'd met a number of women who seemed caring and compassionate. I figured that soon enough I'd know who to ask to sponsor me.

My thoughts weren't that logical at the time. My brain was constantly toying with one idea or another, and I easily became obsessed with whatever mental fodder I found lying around. A storyline around my need to find a boyfriend was a perennial favorite at the time. Just shy of seven years in a loveless marriage, I'd decided I'd grieved long enough. While I'd heard rumblings about not making any drastic changes in the first year of sobriety, that seemed to be excessive. Surely, I was an exception to that rule.

* * *

Sitting on a metal folding chair in the middle of a dingy room was the last place I wanted to be that Monday afternoon. The mid-August heat had thoroughly baked Chicago by then, and the J. Crew suit that helped me blend in at the hospital where I worked was now my straight-jacket (albeit a navy pinstriped one) with some clever name like "The Mason Blazer" or "The Ludlow." I once read in a magazine that navy blue conveyed trustworthiness, and would be an appropriate color if one were to appear in court. A twelve-step recovery meeting seemed like an equally important place to convey honesty. Having gone seven whole days *in a row* without a drop of alcohol, I may not have wanted to be in that chair—but I was superstitious enough to keep my streak going. I couldn't recall the last time I'd gone that long without a drink.

Even though my silk-lined suit was sticking to me, I insisted on having a cup of coffee during the meeting. My hands cradled the Styrofoam cup. The chill that I originally felt coming off the metal folding chair was gone. I kept trying to arrange my flesh in a way that would provide me comfort from a hard surface that had none to offer.

Then a man walked through the door who was so attractive I almost fell out of my chair entirely.

As this presumably sober fellow made his way to the table in the front of the room, he ran his fingers through his long dark hair, pulling it away from his face to reveal a chiseled jaw and moody eyes. He sat down and pushed the folded cuffs of his plaid shirt to reveal forearms covered with tattoos. Unlike the well-orchestrated design found in tattoo sleeves, his forearms were full of tattoos accumulated the hard way: One at a time.

I already had a penchant for wanting to save sad artsy boys. The bonus here was that the reformation work had already been handled for me! Now, I just had to meet him. It was only a matter of time before we'd live happily ever after, and maybe even have some little tattooed babies.

One thing that took me years in recovery to learn was that my initial backstory about people is rarely true. I consider myself a genius when it comes to piecing together context clues, but this is not always accurate—especially when dealing with human beings. The little vignette I'd concocted that afternoon wasn't accurate at all, but it didn't stop me from living in that fantasy world any time I needed a brief respite from reality—which happened frequently, given how raw and exposed I felt without my security blanket of alcohol. Why live in boring old reality, when you can live in your imagination—where you get to control the outcomes?!

I digress...

I learned he'd been sober for seven years, and prior to that he'd been addicted to alcohol and heroin.

He talked about what his life was like now: He prayed, he meditated, he lived with other sober guys. I'm sure he said other things, but I was too busy wondering what his last name was (hoping we would share it one day).

Thank God the men I was attracted to were healthy enough to see I still had a wheelbarrow full of my own emotional work to do. And I was too healthy to tolerate the nonsense that came along with the guys interested in me.

What I can also see now, though, is that I would not have had the freedom to explore the edges of my life in the way that I did had I gotten into a relationship during my first year of sobriety. (Or the seven that followed, if we're keeping track.) I'd spent the first thirty-one years of my life taking someone else's preferences into account. If it wasn't my ex, then it was my mother. I could go out on a limb, sure, but never actually take off from the branch and fly away.

As much as I've railed at the Universe and, on occasion, wallowed in self-pity at the fact that I'm still single when the rest of the world has moved on, I believe on a subconscious level that I'm purposely keeping myself unattached so that when the time is right for me to take flight, there's no risk of someone clipping my wings.

ARE YOU THERE, STEVIE? IT'S ME, STEPHANIE

I cringed when people would use a male pronoun for the concept of a Higher Power. Frankly, I still prefer Higher Power (or its abbreviation "HP") or The Universe to the word "God." Logically, I know the three-letter word is only a signpost, but that particular post has a whole lot of bad blood associated with it. By switching to "HP," I sidestep all that baggage.

I tried to envision HP as something or someone that would symbolize unconditional love and protection, and I preferred a feminine interpretation of the divine. I needed to envision someone to talk to who wasn't so abstract and out of my reach, someone I could imagine having a connection with. So, Stevie Nicks became my concept of a Higher Power, and if I needed to picture someone when asking for help, I pictured speaking directly to her.

My concept of a High Power has shape-shifted over time, and I find it impossible to describe just who or what I'm connecting with; but if I could pin it down, it wouldn't be that powerful a force, now, would it? To this day, hearing Fleetwood Mac pop up on the radio or a playlist feels like kismet—a gentle reminder that I'm not all alone in the world.

Like the sudden flood of fluorescent light in a dive bar at closing time, sobriety has a way of illuminating things that greatly benefit from dim lighting. One unsettling discovery was my own mind's complicity in my pain. I'd prided myself on being intelligent and scrappy—only to learn that my thinking could also work against me?! Working with my mind—to rewire it, essentially—literally became a matter of life and death.

LABELING

To integrate mindfulness practices into my own life, I sought evidence and inspiration anywhere I could find it. Throughout this book, I've woven these gems next to a story that illustrates that particular concept or finding.

SWITCHING FROM MINDLESSNESS
TO MINDFULNESS: LABELING

"Mindlessness sets in when we rely too rigidly on categories and distinctions created in the past (masculine/feminine, old/young, success/failure).

—DR. ELLEN LANGER, PHD[23]

Described as the "mother of mindfulness," Dr. Ellen Langer, PhD, is a social psychologist and the first female professor to gain tenure in the Psychology Department at Harvard University. [24] Over the past thirty-five years, she has written eleven books and over 200 research articles on mindfulness. [25]

In her best-selling book, *Mindfulness*, Dr. Langer exposes the hidden costs of its opposite—mindlessness—and describes the various ways it can occur, including the one she describes in the quote above. [26] One way is through clinging to old labels and definitions, often reflective of the mind's maturity at the time those pronouncements were made.

---

23 Ellen Langer, Ph.D., *Mindfulness* (A Merloyd Lawrence Book, Da Capo Press, 1989), 11.
24 "About," EllenLanger.com (website), Accessed December 26, 2019.
25 Ibid.
26 Ellen Langer, Ph.D., *Mindfulness* (A Merloyd Lawrence Book, Da Capo Press, 1989).

My story of how I challenged and redefined my previous concept of the mental label "God" illustrates the power of being open to creating new categories in our mental model of the world. I've shared the negative associations I had attached to the label "God," as well as my reluctance to open up that mental can of worms— even though the alternative was drinking myself to death. Swapping out my old definition of God (angry grandpa in the sky) for a new one (Stevie Nicks) illustrates the power that labeling things can have over us.

Labeling is neither good nor bad—it's like fire: it can warm you up or burn you. It's all in how you use it. Mindfulness is simply learning how to use your powers for good.

CONNECTING THE DOTS

"Again, you can't connect the dots looking forward; you can only connect them looking backward. So, you have to trust that the dots will somehow connect in your future. You have to trust in something—your gut, destiny, life, karma, whatever. This approach has never let me down, and it has made all the difference in my life."

—STEVE JOBS [27]

---

27 Steve Jobs, Stanford Commencement Address, June 14, 2005, Accessed on December 26, 2019.

On October 5, 2011, Steve Jobs passed away. On my commute to work, just days away from receiving my ninety-day coin, I listened to a National Public Radio (NPR) commentator read excerpts of his Stanford commencement address. In it, Jobs shared about his winding journey to that point in life, and showed how events once perceived as detours and failures led to the very features that were responsible for his success.

Newly divorced and sober, I was still in shock from watching all the dominoes I'd laid so carefully come crashing down into a pattern that looked nothing like I'd intended. I'd lived my life dedicated to the pursuit of what I believed happiness would entail: a career, a husband, material success, children. I envisioned what my holiday card would need to look like in this perfect scenario, and then I reverse engineered the whole thing.

In the same way I bristle at being told what to do or who to be, life instinctively resists my attempts to control it. When the chasm between two dots ended up wider than I'd expected, rather than revise my plan to accommodate reality, I ignored it and spread myself thinner to accommodate the gaps. By prioritizing my designs instead of accepting reality, I repeated this act countless times. Eventually, I spread myself so thin that I snapped under the pressure.

In the aftermath of the physical, emotional, and spiritual destruction that accompanies decades of forcing square pegs into round holes, I had to find a completely new way to approach my life. My familiar façade, the one that proudly declared "I'm winning at life—I've got this" now revealed gigantic cracks and chipping plaster. Not only was my ego worthless to protect me, it became a liability: my mask was drawing even more attention to the damage I'd hoped to conceal by hiding behind it.

So, with Stevie Nicks as my higher power, and Steve Jobs' notion that "eventually the dots would connect," I set out into the big, scary unknown to try to live life one day at a time. More than eight years later, I'm grateful to report that it's still working.

SPOONING THE THIRD RAIL

As I stated earlier, mindfulness practices and the authenticity that results from having a deeper connection to one's True Self do not require any particular type of religious belief system.

Faith is such a controversial topic, I'm reluctant to broach it here; yet, it formed the first major mental hurdle I needed to cross to relinquish control over my life. My egoic self runs on fear, and my fuel supply is abundant. Fortunately, I've found a mental shortcut that has allowed me to continually release the death grip I have on my life's reins. (This notion of control is also an illusion, as the only thing I seem to be able to control are the actions I take and my response to how life unfolds.) If you're looking for air-tight logic—or even a spirited debate on the existence of God—you've come to the wrong place!

If there actually is some sort of God or Higher Power, then why do truly horrible events occur? Both in our personal lives, and on a global scale? How am I supposed to make sense of the Holocaust? I have come to a place where I can accept there are certain events that I will not be able to understand during this lifetime.

Part of my faith—often a significant chunk—is the willingness to flag something I can't fathom and trust that when I die, the authentic eternal spirit that has animated my skin suit during this lifetime will get the opportunity to ask these questions and absorb a greater understanding of how those dots connect. I know logically that, as a human, I am mortal and finite—two attributes that constrain my level of comprehension. My hunch (or hope?) is that when my spirit returns to its source, and I am no longer bound by those constraints, I'll be able to comprehend that which only can be understood by an omniscient and infinite mind.

I'd spent three decades trying to pole vault over that mental bar, and every time I took another run at it, I'd find the bar had been raised. No matter how much higher I could jump, I'd still be unable to clear it. In those first hazy days and weeks of living without alcohol, I realized I could get to the other side by simply walking around it. Rather than beat my brains out trying to reconcile the existence of some sort of benevolent force in the universe with all the injustice I'd experienced, and worse yet, seen inflicted on others, I'm willing to consider that eventually the dots will connect—even if it's not during my time on this planet.

* * *

I've mentioned my numerous qualms with faith, one major reason being that I could not reconcile faith with all the injustice in the world. I still can't—and even that doesn't prevent me from moving through the world as though there might be some power out there greater than myself. If it's useful, here's how I choose to look at it now, so I can enjoy however many moments I have remaining on this planet to their fullest. (Instead of wasting it trying to answer questions that no one has yet been able to answer.)

Some days, that will be enough to pacify my egoic mind. On other days—especially when the pain is not hypothetical, and the person negatively impacted is me—I need to bring in additional mental reinforcements. I share them here in case you find any of them helpful.

WOULD I RATHER BE RIGHT OR HAPPY?

Believing that the dots will connect eventually—even if it won't happen during this lifetime—frees me to take advantage of the comfort that sentiment provides in the meantime.

A dear friend of mine once said, "What if I die and realize this was all made up? Oh well! Joke's on me! At least I got to spend the rest of my life sober."

In this case, holding out for certainty demands a higher price than I'm willing to pay. If someone else finds my logic naive or juvenile, I'm willing to live with that. What they think is none of my business anyway.

BORROWING THE FAITH OF OTHER PEOPLE WHO'VE ALREADY BEEN DOWN THIS ROAD

Anderson Cooper interviewed Stephen Colbert shortly after Cooper's mother, Gloria Vanderbilt, had passed away. During the interview, which aired on August 15, 2019 on CNN, the two men shared a vulnerable exchange regarding pain, grief, and faith, which then went viral. Television critic, Hank Stue-ver, detailed the interview in an article for *The Wall Street Journal*, naming it the best TV moment of the year. [28]

Decades before 9/11 came to symbolize what it does today on a global scale, that September day was already an anniversary of monumental loss for Colbert: his father and brothers died in a plane crash on that date in 1974. [29] As the youngest of eleven, whose older siblings had already moved out of the house, Colbert suddenly found himself living in a once-bustling house that had been reduced to two occupants: His grieving mother and his ten-year-old self.

Stephen Colbert's love of J.R.R. Tolkien's work has been widely publicized through various comedic bits on his television shows. In their interview Anderson Cooper presses Colbert on one such Tolkien reference: "What punishments of God are not gifts?" [30]

Choking up, Cooper asks him, "Do you really believe that?"

Colbert replies, "Yes. It's a gift to exist. And with existence comes suffering. There is no escaping that. I guess I'm either a Catholic or a Buddhist when I say those things. I've heard those from both traditions. But I did not learn it, that I was

---

28 Hank Stuver, "2019's Best TV Moment? It was Stephen Colbert Answering Anderson Cooper's Question About Grief," The Washington Post, December 23, 2019, Accessed on December 26, 2019.

29 Stephen Colbert, interview by Anderson Cooper, *Anderson Cooper 360*, August 15, 2019, Accessed on December 26, 2019.

30 Ibid.

grateful for the thing I most wish hadn't happened...I realized it..."

"It doesn't mean you're happy about it," clarifies Cooper.

"...I want it to not have happened. But if you are grateful for your life...(t)hen you have to be grateful for all of it. You can't pick and choose what you're grateful for," said Colbert. [31]

Colbert goes on to explain that the inherent gift in any form of suffering is the ability to empathize with other people, since suffering is part of the human condition. He attributes weathering such a traumatic experience early on in life as providing him the ability to connect on a deeper level with the important relationships in life now. He is better able to love and understand his wife, his children, and his friends because he can relate to the suffering that all humans experience. [32]

Colbert continues,

"It's about the fullness of your humanity. What's the point of being here and being human?...I want to be the most human I can be and that involves acknowledging and ultimately being grateful for the things that I wish didn't happen, because they gave me a gift." [33]

---

31 Stephen Colbert, interview by Anderson Cooper, *Anderson Cooper 360*, August 15, 2019, Accessed on December 26, 2019.
32 Stephen Colbert, interview by Anderson Cooper, *Anderson Cooper 360*, August 15, 2019, Accessed on December 26, 2019.
33 Ibid.

My own ability to recognize the gift in "God's punishments" (to borrow Tolkien's phrase) has been such a slow one that even time lapse photography would bore a viewer to tears. Only in recent months has my heart been able to open wide enough to acknowledge that human connection is indeed worth the inherent risk involved. The confidence and clarity in Colbert's explanation gives me hope that with additional time and healing, one day I too could be able to realize the same depth of gratitude for suffering in my own life. I'm willing to hang onto his faith until my own faith grows to fill the gap.

CHAPTER 3

GOLD DUST AND THE "W"

———

Growing up, summer camp was my oasis. For six whole days and nights, I was freed from tensions simmering at home and my reputation in elementary school as an awkward geek. At Camp Manitou-Lin, my slate was wiped clean. I got to be myself, and it turned out she loved performing in skits in the mess hall and singing camp songs at the top of her lungs: "Sara, Sara, strong and able, get your elbows off the table!"

Weeks after returning home, I'd inject camp customs into daily life, much to the chagrin of family members when they inadvertently broke one of camp's unspoken rules in my presence. "Grandma, Grandma, strong and able, get your elbows off the table!" Grandma was a good sport, and would laugh and join in with my militant chanting and clapping.

My poor mother, having been subjected to more post-camp meals with me and my newfound voice, pretended not to hear me calling out her elbow violation:

"Becky, Becky, strong and able, get your elbows off the table!"

After repeating myself for a second or third time, she'd lift her gaze above the newspaper and lock eyes with me long enough to signal that her elbows were not going anywhere. At least not until she'd finished reading that section of the *Grand Rapids Press*.

CAMP GROUNDED: SUMMER CAMP FOR ADULTS

I had long forgotten about Camp Manitou-Lin and my repertoire of camp songs, when I stumbled across a video clip on a friend's social media feed advertising Camp Grounded. This summer camp for adults had just finished their inaugural season in the northern California redwoods and was taking registrations for the upcoming season.

The pitch: Spend a long weekend at this summer camp for adults, taking a break from your digitally-connected life and reconnecting to people and yourself, through a return to analog life.

The rules:

No technology. They'd keep phones safely locked up on the premises and return them to us at the end of our Digital Detox.

No "W" talk. Work was a four-letter word, and while we were at camp, we were not to use it as a networking event—or to use our job titles and line of work as filler for those awkward conversations when meeting strangers.

No real names. Similar to Burning Man and other co-created communities, shedding all the associations with our name and identity allowed for that same "clean slate" feeling I'd loved when going to camp as a kid.

No watches/time. The counselors wore watches to keep us to a basic framework for logistical reasons like meal coordination at the mess hall or other scheduled events. Whenever counselors issued instructions about how long we had until the next activity began, time was spoken about in generalities:

"In about the amount of time it takes to boil an egg, we'll be heading to the parade field for the opening ceremony."

Or *"You have an episode of* Game of Thrones *until we'll meet at the campfire."*

By the end of that weekend, my whole body seemed to be in the same state of deep relaxation I'd felt at the end of my first yoga class: It was the late 90s and my default posture for moving through the world was a constricted one, continuously bracing against life's inevitable blows. Lying on the mat in the dimly lit room during the final posture, savasana, my body and my mind were both quiet. At the same time. By the end of that sixty-minute class, I was no longer bound up in knots. I had completely unfurled.

To fit into the cubby assigned for me back in my regular life, I'd contorted myself in numerous ways. While at Camp Grounded, I could be Gold Dust. Not only did the blood flow get restored to my entire body, but my unique edges that normally got stuffed into the mold first were actually celebrated.

Piling back onto the camp buses headed back to San Francisco three days later, I vowed to retain as much of my authentic Gold Dust self back in the "real world" as made sense for me. Yes, I had to return to my "W" which meant using my technology, my watch, and my real name, but the sentiment stayed. In learning how to bring more Gold Dust to my work, and that way I've actually been able to be the best Stephanie that I can be. And that's what this book is about: How to move away from the mindlessness that pervades our daily hyper-connected lives and toward our authentic selves in all areas of our lives, especially our "W."

* * *

Though not fully aware of it at the time, the inner calm that results from a mindful approach to life has always called to me, as evidenced by the euphoria I felt after my first yoga class.

If this book appeals to you, I suspect you have similar experiences, even though you may not have labeled them "mindfulness practices." The activities and methods that get us out of ourselves—out of a state of mindlessness—vary depending on our preferences.

For me, painting, writing, meditation, and yoga are the main methods I use to practice mindfulness. I don't always reach a "flow" state every time I do them (especially with seated meditation—for me, that is the least "flow-like" of them all.) While interviewing people for this book, I found people who achieved these same benefits through a number of other activities, including surfing, running, and working out.

I'm of the opinion that it doesn't matter **how** I get out of my head and into the present moment, it's simply **that** I do it.

Similarly, my ability to stay out of my head varies greatly. In the beginning, I would judge myself harshly for not being able to achieve a certain quality or quantity of stillness.

Over time, I've realized that the benefit seems to come from flexing the muscle of routine: It's sitting down to write my morning pages that matters—not how much "zen" I can wring out of them. No matter how my particular type of practice goes, I still accumulate the associated benefits: increasingly I am able to catch myself before automatically reacting to a challenging situation. That brief pause—the gap between thought and action—gives me freedom to choose a different response. And to grow closer to being the best possible version of myself.

I AM NOT A GURU

I am not a mindfulness guru. I'm a self-taught practitioner and a proponent of the results mindfulness produces. I fundamentally rebel against the notion that an intermediary is required for this type of work. I've taken meditation classes, read numerous books on the subject, downloaded various mindfulness apps, and breathed along with them (both with and without a paid subscription). I am grateful for the various teachers, authors, and application designers that have helped me carve my own path toward mindfulness, but my ability to connect to my authentic self is not dependent on any one of them.

The single most important facet of mindfulness training is our own personal experience of learning how to observe our thoughts instead of getting caught up in them. I can read every book and article ever written about surfing, but that will still not make me a surfer. There's no substitute for time spent in the ocean trying to get up on a board and ride it.

Ironically, my authority on this topic rests on my complete lack of credentials. These tools are open and available to anyone who seeks them. This book will focus primarily on experiences, both others' and my own, as opposed to theory.

However, theory is incredibly valuable! As you go through this book, you'll find my own application of theory to the ideas expressed in others' stories and my own. I encourage you to think of this book as a jumping off point for your own exploration—seeking out the authors and resources mentioned here and in the bibliography as additional cosmic bread crumbs for you to follow on your own journey.

Most importantly, I want to stress that I am only an authority on my own experience—not on yours. Yes, I am Gold Dust. But remember: You are too.

QUIETING MY EGO HELPS MY AUTHENTIC SELF SHINE
As I mentioned earlier, this book covers topics that are squishy enough in nature. Here is one more review of the common terms I use, and how I define them.

Again, the term **ego** can be used in multiple ways. I think of it as the near-continuous chatter in my brain, providing color commentary (both positive and negative) as I move throughout the world. This internal narration is one of the numerous tactics my ego uses to regulate my self-esteem. The narration is an attempt to help me feel more in control of my surroundings (even though whatever sense of control I have is an illusion).

If pressed to select a more scientific definition, my definition of ego most closely aligns to the concept of unchecked egotism and its more desirable counterpart, the quiet ego, defined by Jack J. Bauer and Heidi A. Wayment: "the quiet ego and quieting the ego...connote the individual who routinely transcends egotism as well as the need to turn down a few notches the booming volume of egotism, on both individual and cultural levels." [34]

Mindfulness is the ability to notice thought patterns and redirect my attention to those that support the best version of myself. Mindfulness practices help me quiet the ego.

My ego resists any attempt at mindfulness, because mindfulness practices threaten my ego's existence. As such, I can't stress the following point enough: *Rather than debate the merits of one particular mindfulness practice over another, my view is that it doesn't matter **how** we get out of our heads and into the present moment, it's simply **that** we do it.*

---

34   Jack J. Bauer & Heidi A. Wayment, "The psychology of the quiet ego" in Decade of Behavior. Transcending Self-Interest: Psychological Explorations of the Quiet Ego, eds. H. A. Wayment & J. J. Bauer, (Washington, D.C.: American Psychological Association, 2008), 7–19.

Mindlessness is the opposite of mindfulness: having no distinction between my thoughts and my reality. In a mindless state, I'm going through life on autopilot, with my unobserved brain providing the algorithm, often in a state of unchecked egotism.

Authenticity is acting from my true self regardless of the setting. By setting appropriate and flexible boundaries, I am still able to choose how little or how much of my *authentic self* (or *best self*) I share in a given setting, depending on the situation and the level of trust I have with the person, people, or institution concerned. I rely on my *inner compass* (my *intuition*) to guide the location and rigidity of those boundaries, which may be revised over time to suit a relationship's particular needs.

Writing for *Scientific American*, Columbia psychologist, Scott Barry Kaufman, explains that the ego's obsession with self-preservation actually inhibits its ability to achieve its most pressing goals. [35] Building off the empirical evidence backing Wayment and her colleagues' work, Kaufman asserts what I've found to be true in my personal experience:

These results underscore the centrality of growth and balance values to the quiet ego construct, and make clear that quieting the ego does not quiet the self. In fact, I would like to put forward the following equation:

The quieter the ego = The stronger one's best self emerges. [36]

---

35 Scott Barry Kaufman, Ph.D., "The Pressing Need for Everyone to Quiet Their Egos," *Scientific American*, May 21, 2018, Accessed on December 21, 2019.

36 Ibid.

Through the use of mindfulness practices to quiet my ego, I have become my most authentic, "Gold Dust"-y self, in all areas of my life, including the workplace. Being true to my authentic self, instead of hiding behind my usual masks has required vulnerability, but the reward of leaving that self-protective armor behind is beyond worth it: I now have deeper, more meaningful connections with people in all areas of my life, including the workplace. (In fact, many of my colleagues helped fund the publication of the first edition of this book.)

SOUND-PROOFING THE SELF-ZOO

I find it comforting that even academics use words associated with noise and volume to describe the nature of the ego. The cacophony in my head might be intense, but at least I'm not the only one trying to function with a loud mind.

Abraham Tesser, a professor and researcher at the William A. and Barbara R. Owens Institute for Behavioral Research at the University of Georgia, and his colleagues explored the myriad ways the ego protects itself, all with the same goal of preserving self-esteem. [37] Tesser et al labeled these tactics the "self-zoo of self-defense mechanisms," in that the ego had a menagerie of ways to continually monitor and repair one's self-esteem in response to the feedback life continually provides. [38]

---

37   Tesser, Ph.D., Abraham, "On the Plasticity of Self-Defense," *Current Directions in Psychological Science* 10, no. 2, April 2001):66–69.
38   Abraham et al., "Confluence of Self-Esteem Regulation Mechanisms: On Integrating the Self-Zoo," *Personality and Social Psychology Bulletin*, 26 no. 12 (November 2000): 1476–1489.

By contrast, Bauer and Wayment's work outlines the characteristics of a quiet ego: [39]

- wisdom
- altruism
- sense of interdependence with all living things
- more comfort with life's gray areas (i.e., not stuck in "black and white" patterns of thinking)
- less prone to anger and/or episodes of verbal aggression
- less prone to view life through a negative lens

In a study of adults with various backgrounds of exposure to mindfulness and Buddhist practices, Wayment's research showed that meditating on a regular basis and experience with Buddhism resulted in increased psychological mindfulness scores, which were correlated with the quiet ego traits listed above. [40] Quiet ego characteristics are linked to higher self-reported health outcomes, reinforcing the physical and psychological benefits of mindfulness practices. [41]

---

39 Jack J. Bauer & Heidi A. Wayment, "The psychology of the quiet ego" in Decade of Behavior. Transcending Self-Interest: Psychological Explorations of the Quiet Ego, eds. H. A. Wayment & J. J. Bauer, (Washington, D.C.: American Psychological Association, 2008), 7–19.

40 Heidi A. Wayment, Ph.D., et al., "Doing and Being: Mindfulness, Health, and Quiet Ego Characteristics Among Buddhist Practitioners," Journal of Happiness Studies 12, no. 4, (July 2010):575–589.

41 Ibid.

THERE'S NO SUBSTITUTE FOR PRACTICE

Knowing the *why* behind the *what* helps me make sense of my world, which is why you'll find applicable theories throughout this book. My main focus, however, will be to keep us oriented toward action. We will only derive the actual benefits of quieting our egoic mind by incorporating these practices into our own lives. Simply reading and talking about mindfulness defeats the purpose. Instead of moving closer toward our authentic selves, we're bolstering our egos by congratulating ourselves for all the additional knowledge we've accumulated.

It's like setting out to renovate a house, and rather than ripping down a wall like I'd planned, I read a book on wall demolition, printed myself a certificate of completion, framed it, and hung it on the aforementioned wall. I accomplished a few things (reading a book, making, framing, and hanging my DIY certificate), but instead of being closer toward my actual goal (ripping down the wall) I'm further away than when I started.

Full disclosure: Ego bolstering and certificate creation happen to the best of us, myself included. Our goal is to recognize when it's happening, roll up our sleeves, and get back to work dismantling this barrier that's keeping us from our authentic selves—and ultimately, connecting with each other.

TAKE WHAT YOU LIKE AND LEAVE THE REST

"When you are too sure about God and faith, you are sure of something other than God: of dogma, of the church, of a particular interpretation of the Bible. But God cannot be pigeonholed. We must press toward certainty, but be suspicious when it comes too glibly."

—STAN WEIRSMA, IN A LETTER FROM ENGLAND IN 1973 TO A YOUNGER COLLEAGUE, HARMON HOOK [42]

Mindfulness does not require any particular set of beliefs. The mindsets and tools included in this book work regardless of whether you are a devout follower of a specific religious tradition, agnostic, atheistic, or anywhere in between.

While sharing my personal experiences (i.e. getting sober) and beliefs (i.e. my views on spirituality) may be off-putting to some readers, it seemed the only way to illustrate the dramatic change mindfulness, and the resulting authenticity, had in my life.

If you're still with me, wonderful. If my particular viewpoint is bothering you, *even better!* By sitting with the discomfort these words are triggering within you, you're already applying these mindfulness tools to your life.

---

42 Stan Weirsma, qtd. in a program for the Eleventh Annual Wiersma Memorial Lecture, Calvin College Festival of Faith and Writing, 2000.

I've included my own feelings (both emotions and physical body sensations) to give you the most complete picture of my own experience walking through the world in this way. By no means am I suggesting that my way is:

- Typical
- The "only" way
- The preferable way

Dogma has caused enough pain and suffering in the world. I don't want to further contribute to separation among human beings. My goal is connection: To find those places on a Venn diagram where my circle and your circle overlap.

PART 2

FOLLOWING THE COSMIC BREAD CRUMBS

CHAPTER 4

MINDFULNESS PRACTICES: START EXPLORING AND KEEP EVOLVING

———

"At the center of your being you have the answer; you know who you are and you know what you want."

—LAO TZU [43]

I can't tell you what your version of "Gold Dust" is. No one can.

The good news is, you already know. Whether you're consciously aware of it or not, your authentic self is on and

---

43   Tzu, Lao Qtd. In "Lao Tzu: Quotable Quotes." Goodreads (website). Accessed December 20, 2019.

sending out signals to direct you where you need to go. The challenge is in learning how to tune into those frequencies and ignore all the other stimuli competing for your attention. Which brings us to the topic of developing a mindfulness practice that works for you. I'll elaborate on mindfulness practices that have helped myself and others make and foster that connection with our authentic selves, but only you will be able to figure out what works for you.

MY MINDFULNESS PRACTICE: HUMBLE BEGINNINGS

My introduction to the world of "mindfulness" was more of a crash course in how to stave off insanity: Desperate to slow down the hamster wheel spinning in my brain, it actually made it easier to follow suggestions that I doubted would have any impact at all.

At the beginning, my mindfulness practice included three basic components:

- Meditation: The most I could handle was setting a timer for six minutes, and trying not to open my eyes during that time.
- Reading: I'd read a page out of a "thought for the day" type book for people in recovery
- Prayer: I'd recite some prayers to Stevie Nicks that my sponsor had suggested.

In the beginning, my motivation was 99 percent superstition and 1 percent belief that someone or something was listening. Truthfully, my belief-o-meter usually hovers between 17 percent and 39 percent. It's those bizarre coincidences and the astounding "before and after" differences resulting from this work that keeps me in the routine of doing it. I do it because it makes me feel better.

Again: Beliefs are completely optional! My views could best be described as spiritual, but not religious; however, please don't let my concept of spirituality (or anyone else's, for that matter) get in the way of you connecting to your authentic self.

* * *

I'd already been incorporating mindfulness practices in my life for three years when I boarded that flight to San Francisco International Airport, en route to my first trip to Camp Grounded. While Camp Grounded would help me get reacquainted with my authentic self—Gold Dust—I'd already removed a number of the masks I'd previously used to keep myself hidden.

I'd experienced the most stark contrast of living a double life at the end of my marriage and drinking career. Here's what that disconnect looked like:

When the alarm blared at 5:00 a.m., I'd roll out of bed (literally—our Tempurpedic mattress was on the floor of that apartment) and shut it off, so as not to wake my ex.

Things were so bleak that I'd begun using cigarettes as a bribe for getting out of bed. My refusal to get up in the mornings had turned my relationship with the snooze button into one that closely mimicked Chinese water torture: I'd sacrifice an hour of sleep for repeated nine-minute increments of drifting in and out of a consciousness I desperately wished not to be real.

Since my mental tug of war also disturbed my then-husband's sleep, I devised a solution. In exchange for immediately getting out of bed to face another day, I could extend my closet smoking habit to the early morning hours. Granted, my drink of choice would have to be coffee (instead of gin and tonic), but I'd still get those quiet moments to myself before having to suit up for another day of spinning plates and tap dancing fast enough to keep everyone around me happy.

By the time I left for Camp Grounded, I hadn't experienced mornings like that in over four years. Our divorce was finalized on June 23, 2011. My final drag off a cigarette happened that July. August 8, 2011, is my first (and hopefully my only) sobriety date. The physical, emotional, and spiritual healing that took place over the next few years provided the groundwork that allowed me to connect with my authentic self, Gold Dust, the way I later did at Camp Grounded in May of 2014.

This is a slow process, and one that's unique to each of us. By no means should my experience be a benchmark—I'm describing it here to illustrate the nature of this work: nonlinear and constantly evolving.

MY MINDFULNESS PRACTICE: AN EVOLUTION

By 2014, my mornings had evolved to include a mindfulness practice that looks similar to the one I use now. I usually wake up before my alarm, and spend an hour connecting to my authentic self. (Please note: I didn't start off spending this much time getting grounded before heading out into my day!)

My morning practice evolves as I need it to. I began experimenting with meditation apps and timers. I added additional "page a day" books to my repertoire. I began writing "Morning Pages" as outlined in Julia Cameron's *The Artist's Way*.[44] Part of a larger twelve-week process to heal and clear creative blocks, "Morning Pages" are simply three pages of stream of consciousness writing. I've found this practice to be my most effective method for maintaining something resembling a Quiet Ego state.

Several of the people interviewed for this book mentioned the use of Morning Pages when asked about their current mindfulness practices. Similarly, a number of people mentioned using gratitude lists (writing out a list of what you're grateful for) as well. Physical activities, especially ones that require focused attention to execute them correctly (like surfing, power lifting, and CrossFit) are also effective.

I don't know that a gym would be my first response when listing off places to practice mindfulness, but Crossfit Defined—and by extension the coaches and community of athletes—has played a critical piece of my own development since I joined in November of 2017. While I've been in recovery from an eating disorder (bulimia) since September 1, 2013, I still have some old stories rattling around in my head about

---

44   Julia Cameron, *The Artist's Way: A Spiritual Path to Higher Creativity*, (New York, Penguin Putnam Inc.), 1992, 9–24.

my lack of athletic ability, what my body should look like, etc. Being in a class with athletes of all different shapes, sizes, and fitness levels can send me spiraling.

Thanks to quality coaching and an inclusive community vibe, Crossfit Defined has taught me how to "get comfortable with being uncomfortable." In my body, I've found activities that get me out of my comfort zone and promote mindfulness via different means than my more solitary, inward morning practices.

The two vastly different styles of practicing mindfulness complement each other. My standard solitary reflective practices allow me to access what bubbles up when there's nothing to distract me from myself.

On the other end of the spectrum, there's the rigorous physical nature of a CrossFit or strength training workout, with an added communal component. My ego reacts when it's challenged in this sort of environment, where it has a heightened perception of being threatened. As long as I'm observing what's happening (versus getting sucked into the storyline) I'm gaining additional feedback that informs my inner work, helping me further dismantle my defense mechanisms. Had I only used mindfulness practices that played to my strengths, it's likely these barriers would have gone undetected and unchallenged.

I interviewed David Sutor, co-owner of Crossfit Defined and one of my coaches. The mental aspects of effective coaching are just as important as the physical movements. During the two and a half years I've trained there, I've noticed parallels between my own work on mindfulness and its application in the gym, (i.e., performance improvement, behavioral modification, etc.).

When I asked about any practices he uses to keep his ego in check, his answer surprised me. I knew his strength and conditioning sessions (which occur four times a week on average) would make the list. He surprised me by leading off with a recent shift he experienced as a result of completing a weekly self-appraisal that included a gratitude list. He explained,

"For the past five or six years, I've woken up feeling like I just don't have enough time, like l should have been up thirty minutes earlier—basically just feeling *behind*."

As part of a twelve-week personal development coaching engagement, David was asked to complete an online form, recapping his week. He spent a half hour answering various self-reflection questions, including writing out a gratitude list. After only two weeks, he already noticed a dramatic improvement—when he woke up, the anxiety was gone.

"Now I wake up with peace. *I wake up with no anxiety!*"

He continued the practice for the duration of the twelve weeks, and found the benefits continued to expand.

Dumbfounded by both the simplicity and the efficacy of the gratitude list and identifying goals for the upcoming week, David now views this weekly self-reflection, gratitude, and goal-setting as a nonnegotiable part of his routine. He's considering minor adjustments to personalize it and that make it feel more like a ritual (e.g., adding questions, going to a coffee shop specifically for the purpose of filling it out, etc.).

The other nonnegotiable? I'll let him explain:

"Training. It's my meditation, man. My phone doesn't matter. Bills don't matter. The stress at work doesn't matter...for an hour to an hour and a half, that's my peace. It's my calm. It's the whole thing. I feel better."

He compares his workouts to a devout parishioner's experience of church. The playful banter among the people he's lifting with that day fulfills the same role as the sermon. Having seen these exchanges in person, the nature of the shit-talking is clearly meant for motivational purposes only.

Just like church, the gym also provides fellowship. David describes the challenge of a being an alpha leading a team of alphas, and for the first time I reflect on how unusual it is that there haven't been monumental clashes of wills. Perhaps these are confined to only those involved in them. My sense is that the importance of the community—which Crossfit Defined clearly is—overrides the importance of appeasing any particular ego that feels threatened at the time.

If training is a form of devotion, Dwayne Johnson is certainly a believer.

In *First Hand: The Rock's Philosophy, As Told Through His Own Two Hands*, the wrestling legend-turned action star, entrepreneur, and Hollywood mogul recounts a pivotal moment in his origin story: After being evicted from their efficiency and forced to leave the island of Hawaii, Dwayne Johnson couldn't bear to watch his mother break down because their family had no place to live. He was only fourteen, but he was determined never to be that helpless again. [45]

"I realized then, that in life, there's a lot of things that I feel we can't control. I can't control what anybody says or does. I can't control Mother Nature...I can't control God's way, God's will, The Universe's way—when it wants something to happen. But certainly, I can control the work that I put in with my two hands, and this idea has served me pretty (well) over the years," Johnson explains. [46]

Dwayne Johnson often weaves the concept of "mana" (the Hawaiian word for spirit) into his observations on life. He writes,

"'Warrior mana' is my foundation…My mana is my DNA that keeps me grounded and hungry. Find your 'mana' and let it lead you. Inspire you…to be a little better today than you were yesterday." [47]

If Gold Dust feels a little feminine for you, perhaps Warrior Mana will better align with your energetic preferences.

---

45 Barbara Anastacio, "First Hand: The Rock's Philosophy, As Told Through His Own Two Hands," *The Wall Street Journal,* (Online), December 3, 2019, Accessed on January 11, 2020.

46 Barbara Anastacio, "First Hand: The Rock's Philosophy, As Told Through His Own Two Hands," *The Wall Street Journal,* (Online), December 3, 2019, Accessed on January 11, 2020.

47 Dwayne Johnson, Facebook post, March 19, 2015, Accessed on January 27, 2020.

In a talk given as part of the Los Angeles Lakers Genius Series, Johnson explains the importance of grounding his aspirations and thought processes. He acknowledges that ambitions are important, but they must connect to something larger, and for Johnson, that anchor is his dedication putting in the work, specifically his time spent training, every day.

To the auditorium of elite athletes in front of him, Johnson says,

"The anchor is getting up at 4 o'clock in the morning every day before anyone else and grounding my thought processes in the (idea that) 'no one will outwork me. No one.' I love and I respect you guys. You (expletive) won't outwork me." [48]

His reputation for his incredible work ethic, combined with gratitude and positivity, are evident not just in the finished products of his work and the success of his business ventures, but in the daily glimpses into his life via social media that consistently reinforce messages of gratitude, service, and perseverance.

Josh Eells' interview with Johnson featured in the *Wall Street Journal* explores the success Johnson enjoys as a result of being a "suit who doesn't seem like one." [49] With a social media following of 232 million across Instagram, Facebook,

48 Dwayne Johnson, MotivationHub, "Dwayne 'The Rock' Johnson's Speech Will Leave You Speechless - One of the Most Eye Opening Speeches," August 7, 2018, Accessed January 3, 2020.

49 Josh Eells, "The Rock, From Strength to Strength," *The Wall Street Journal*, (Online), December 3, 2019, Accessed on December 9, 2019.

and Twitter (the size of a large country, Eells notes), a critic could argue that this is the result of the most sophisticated PR campaign ever executed. In fact, Eells notes that fans either "don't realize they're being sold to, or they don't care." [50]

My view is that everyone is trying to sell me something—it may not be a product, and they may not even be aware that they're doing it—but my job is to discern for myself whether each bit of information I consume is true or not, and whether I choose to absorb it.

Aside from my intuition and the abundance of examples I can point to that have reinforced my belief, it's the relationship he appears to have with his ex-wife that seems impossible to fake. Dany Garcia, a powerhouse within her own right, is the co-CEO of Seven Bucks Productions, the company Johnson named after the amount of money he had to his name when his hopes at a football career were permanently dashed. [51]

Tom Rothman, chairman of Sony Pictures Motion Picture Group, echoes this sentiment:

"He's a genuinely good dude—and the audience can tell. I would wager that no matter how many people you talk to, you won't find a person who will say one ill word about Dwayne Johnson. And you absolutely cannot fake that in life. That means that's who you are." [52]

---

50   Ibid.
51   Josh Eells, "The Rock, From Strength to Strength," *The Wall Street Journal*, (Online), December 3, 2019, Accessed on December 9, 2019.
52   Ibid.

THE RIPPLE EFFECT: HOW MINDFULNESS LEADS TO AUTHENTICITY

What we're looking for is, over time, a slight pause between stimulus and response—a split second or more, where you have the choice to handle a situation differently. The times that validate my own work in this area come in those moments when I catch myself responding in a way that is far more enlightened and kinder than the reaction the same stimulus would have produced in me several years, or months, earlier.

Before getting to that state, however, things usually get worse before they get better. This is why so many of us stay distracted and only partially awake: To avoid the inevitable change we'd have to accept if we allowed ourselves to experience the truth of our reality.

If you begin wandering down this path toward mindfulness, and notice some uncomfortable truths bubbling to the surface—don't panic—everything is happening as it should. You're right on time.

CHAPTER 5

IN PRAISE OF THE PUPA

—

"The psyche knows how to heal, but it hurts. Sometimes the healing hurts more than the initial injury, but if you can survive it, you'll be stronger, because you've found a larger base."

—JOSEPH CAMPBELL [53]

"Just when the caterpillar thought its life was over, it became a butterfly."

—ANONYMOUS

---

53 Joseph Campbell, *A Joseph Campbell Companion: Reflections on the Art of Living*, Eds. Joseph Campbell, Robert Walter, David Kudler, San Anselmo, CA: Joseph Campbell Foundation, 2011, Kindle location 321.

COMPLETE METAMORPHOSIS

All butterflies experience four distinct stages on their way to becoming an adult: the egg, larva, pupa, and adult. This process, called a "complete metamorphosis," differs from the "incomplete metamorphosis" where the nymphs essentially look like adults, just smaller and lack wings (e.g., grasshoppers or dragonflies). [54]

It may be a bit hackneyed, but I have a soft spot for metaphors involving butterflies. While my Gold Dust alter ego has a flower crown that, in addition to silk daisies, includes a faux butterfly as well, the pupa stage is actually the one I identify with most: Inside the chrysalis, the caterpillar begins digesting itself.

Writing for *Scientific American*, Ferris Jabr describes both the chaos and the order involved in this process, all of which are completely hidden beneath the surface.

First, the caterpillar digests itself, releasing enzymes to dissolve all of its tissues. If you were to cut open a cocoon or chrysalis at just the right time, caterpillar soup would ooze out. But the contents of the pupa are not entirely an amorphous mess.... Before hatching, when a caterpillar is still developing inside its egg, it grows an imaginal disc for each of the adult body parts it will need as a mature butterfly or moth...Once a caterpillar has disintegrated all of its tissues except for the imaginal discs, those discs use the protein-rich soup all around them to fuel the rapid cell division required to form the wings, antennae,

---

54 The Academy of Natural Sciences of Drexel University, "Butterfly Life Cycle," ANSP.org (website), Accessed on January 4, 2020.

legs, eyes, genitals, and all the other features of an adult but-
terfly or moth. [55]

Radical change involves construction and destruction. In my experience, there's also been a lengthy period in between the "before" and "after" pictures. This is part of the deceptive appeal of makeover photos or movie montages: as viewers, we get the instant gratification of the "after" picture, with the benefit of hindsight, and none of that messy, awkward time in between, where it's not clear that all the time, effort, money, confusion, is actually going to produce anything of value. If I had to choose, this is why I'd side with #TeamPupa.

ANTHONY COZZI

Anthony's story begins during an initial falling apart phase in the early 2000s, when he was struggling to kick his addiction to heroin and alcohol. Growing up on the South Side of Chicago, his father was a Union worker, like most of the other fathers in this working-class community. Watching his oldest son self-destruct, there was nothing he could do to help, but when he heard one of the unions was hiring, he mentioned the opportunity. In a gruff, yet loving way he told his son,

"If you're not going to do anything with your life, you might as well go sign up for the bricklayers union. At least you'll have a job for the rest of your life."

---

55   Ferris Jabr, "How Does a Caterpillar Turn into a Butterfly?" *Scientific American*, August 10, 2012, Accessed on January 4, 2020.

It would take Anthony four years to finally get sober, but during that time, he cobbled together enough training in the pre-apprenticeship program, so that when he did get clean and sober, he was able to get a job. Over the next seven years, in addition to his job as a bricklayer, he went back to school and earned a degree from Columbia College. He began making music again, reviving yet another aspect of himself that had atrophied while he was in active addiction. He began booking shows for a local club, and formed several bands.

Continuing to apply himself to his trade, he eventually completed the five-year apprenticeship required to join the bricklayers union. He specialized in restoration masonry, a metaphor for the work he'd put into rehabilitating his own life. This particular type of masonry, similar to life in recovery, came with its share of risks.

Anthony explains,

"It was a good job, but very, very dangerous. I would be hanging off the side of 800-foot buildings above downtown Chicago...I often feared for my life, (asking himself) 'Is today the day I'm going to lose an arm or fall off the scaffold?'"

The work environment no longer fit the person he was becoming. Recovery demands soft skills, like vulnerability and accepting one's feelings, that are a stark contrast to the bravado and constant hazing that were accepted standards on the worksites. In addition to the risks to his physical and emotional safety, he also feared that he might miss the opportunity to do the things he really wanted to do with his life.

The plummeting Chicago temperatures each winter meant seasonal layoffs for the bricklayers union. After a particularly depressing off-season, when spring arrived Anthony couldn't bring himself to call the boss and go back to work. In addition to that, his band broke up and his relationship with his girlfriend ended.

He explains, "I was kind of just left with myself. And I wasn't really happy with the person that I was."

He dug back into the spiritual work of twelve-step recovery to once again find the inner peace he'd experienced when he first got sober. This work included going to meetings, working with a sponsor and passing what he'd learned through his experiences by sponsoring other men.

Reflecting on my own experience in recovery, I picture it as being one link in an energetic chain: no better or worse than anyone else, and keeping my connection to this lifeline by passing along what was given to me. I also find that my dedication to spiritual growth ebbs and flows: I have to accept that course corrections are a natural part of being on this journey.

Though I can only see it in hindsight, I find the valleys are critical to producing the change necessary to reach another peak. Until I hit bottom, I was not ready to do the difficult emotional work to live life without anesthesia. Ignoring problematic thought or behavior patterns eventually causes me pain. That pain motivates me to try something different, and sit with the discomfort that comes with implementing a new behavior.

My tolerance for pain has decreased over the years, and I am more proactive about putting in my spiritual work; however, even when things are going very well, my dedication comes from pain avoidance—not virtue.

WHEN THE STUDENT IS READY, THE TEACHER WILL APPEAR

In Anthony's case, the emotional tilling that accompanies spiritual work created the ideal conditions for new growth. Synchronicity began to occur: A friend gave him Joseph Campbell's *The Hero with a Thousand Faces* and Netflix began streaming *Joseph Campbell: Mythos*.

Campbell's use of modern psychology and comparative mythology to explain how humans relate to themselves transformed Anthony's outlook. Like me, Anthony had strong prejudices against world religions and the idea of God. Campbell's approach shattered those rock-solid beliefs, making space for a new conception of himself and his role in this world.

He explains,

"It totally opened up (a) new way of thinking and relating to myself and the world. (Campbell) talked about the hero's journey [essentially] 'the road less traveled'....The traveled road is the one where your parents and society define your life...you go to school, get a degree, get a job that you don't really like, but that will give you a comfortable life. But there's no passion."

Anthony intuitively knew that he needed to follow his passion to be fulfilled. He explains,

"If I am doing the thing that I love to do, and that is supporting my life, I'm being of service to the world. I'm living in my own truth. I'm being the best version of myself I can be, and hopefully, that will inspire someone else to do the same."

THE BUTTERFLY ONLY HAS TO EXPERIENCE THE PUPA PHASE ONCE

Unlike the butterfly, our evolution continues. Just because I've earned my wings once, doesn't mean I won't undergo another prolonged session (or seven) inside the chrysalis.

It's helpful for me to be reminded that some seasons of life will feel more like caterpillar stew than others. While I know growth is not linear, it often seems like it should be. I'm exactly where I'm supposed to be: I may have to experience certain lessons multiple times, from various viewpoints, to (once again) emerge with my wings intact.

Once Anthony realized his need to incorporate more of the activities that brought him joy (heeding Joseph Campbell's advice to follow one's bliss), he began focusing on his music again, and began touring more. Positive changes continued to occur, and life began to get more interesting. In the back of his mind, Anthony had toyed with the idea of moving out to California for several years, but nothing ever really came of it.

Sometimes these patterns take a while to resurface, but if we look carefully, we will begin to notice that life begins to change in ways that serve to nudge us closer toward the life we insist we want. In April of 2015, his ties to Chicago began to unravel, one by one. Soon, the only remaining tie he had to Chicago was his band Radar Eyes, which he loved. Then the guitarist announced he was leaving the band.

"I finally had this band that I really loved," Anthony recalls. "I loved everything we were doing, and I quit, and it was the last thing that was holding me to Chicago."

After venting frustrations he'd discussed numerous times with his sponsor, Anthony recalls the loving, but stern, guidance he received: "I want you to sell everything you own and move (to LA) tomorrow. I completely support you, but I won't talk to you about this again."

While Anthony didn't leave town the next day, he did make up his mind to move. Several months later, he sold everything he owned, packed up his car, and at forty years old, with no job, and only a temporary place to stay, he set out for L.A. You can hear the exhilaration in his voice as he remembers making that leap:

"I can't tell you the level of freedom I had when I was driving out here! It was like something out of a fucking movie. It took two days, driving sixteen to eighteen hours a day. There was no sightseeing, no meandering."

He drove straight to his parent's house in Phoenix and collapsed for two days. After spending a few days with his family, he completed the final leg of his journey, arriving in L.A.

Suddenly, he found himself asking, "Why did I do this? Why am I here?"

He set about building his new life on the west coast. He began working at a yoga studio, and a record store. The jobs didn't pay well, but both work environments were more suited to his interests. He got into a relationship and started playing with several bands.

After a while, he began to experience the same kind of falling away that precipitated his move to L.A.: his relationship ended; he wasn't a good fit for the bands he was playing in, so he left them; and he needed to make more money to cover the increased cost of living compared with Chicago.

As he noticed the familiar pattern beginning to repeat itself, Anthony felt trapped, similar to Bill Murray's experience in the movie *Groundhog Day*. In my own life, it's usually the realization of a pattern—my own version of the *Groundhog Day* scenario—that alerts me to the fact that I need to change.

Acknowledging that he had just lived through the California version of the same events that transpired before he left Chicago, Anthony turned the focus inward to address the root of the problem: the problems manifesting in the material world seemed to be a symptom of inner turmoil.

The details of our stories are different, but the pattern of things falling apart, and then coming back together, and then falling apart again mirror each other. Once I recognize the pattern, I become more willing to pursue spiritual solutions instead of treating the external symptoms. My ability to be mindful is directly linked to my ability to recognize a pattern and generate the willingness to address what needs to be changed.

Anthony dug back into the spiritual work of connecting to his authentic self. He took a break from dating, and committed himself to doing The Artist's Way. He began working with a coach to help him rewrite some of the old stories in his head, related to relationships and his self-worth.

His time inside the chrysalis continues to yield positive results: He started his own construction and renovation company, which allows him the flexibility in his schedule to write music, play shows, and DJ. Anthony Cozzi, and his creativity, are both thriving.

WHEREVER YOU GO, THERE YOU ARE

When life becomes uncomfortable, it's easy to fall for the trap that once the problem at hand is corrected, I will feel better—and life will actually be better.

Toward the end of my time at the tech startup, my soul was twisted in knots: I sensed my work environment was a toxic one, but I loved the actual work I was doing. More importantly, I didn't quite trust my ability to separate my ego from my instincts: What if the workplace only seemed toxic to me because they weren't doing things "my" way?

Then again, I kept seeing evidence that my gut instincts were right and the people in charge had a vested interest in looking the other way. I fantasized about how great it would feel to leave that place, and when recruiters reached out to me, I entertained their offers. By this point, I'd seen enough evidence to trust that when the time was right, I'd be shown what to do.

In the meantime, I followed the suggestion to do my best to stay in the "hula hoop of now," a.k.a., the present moment.

Unfortunately, my "present" ranged from "uncomfortable" to "excruciating." Desperate for relief, and already having made the adjustments to my medication, sleep, diet, and exercise recommended by the professionals on my care team, I begrudgingly sought additional spiritual solutions.

LEARNING TO STAY IN THE PRESENT MOMENT

I began working with my own mindfulness practices even more diligently, expanding beyond the practices that had helped me for the first few years of my sobriety. Here are several of the resources I found exceptionally helpful, and which I continue to return to when difficult situations arise.

Pema Chödrön

Don't Bite the Hook: Finding Freedom from Anger, Resentment, and Other Destructive Emotions

When Pain Is the Doorway: Awakening in the Most Difficult Circumstances

Ekhart Tolle

The Power of Now: A Guide to Spiritual Enlightenment

A New Earth: Awakening to Your Life's Purpose

Michael Singer

The Untethered Soul: The Journey Beyond Yourself

Marianne Williamson

A Return to Love: Reflections on the Principles of a Course in Miracles

I kept asking the Universe to show me what to do about whether or not I should leave that company, but the response remained the same. (I never consulted a Magic Eight Ball, but if it had the answer, it would have been some version of "Ask Again Later.")

After a particularly painful department-wide meeting, I approached Stevie Nicks for guidance and I didn't hold back. My actual request to The Universe went like this:

"Look, you and I both know that I can gut out anything. So, whatever you want me to do here, I need you to make it crystal clear."

Within forty-eight hours, I was informed that the entire strategy department where I worked had been cut and my services were no longer needed.

Once the shock wore off, my initial assumption proved correct: The pain of being in that toxic environment was alleviated.

Burnt out and questioning the broader direction of my career, I decided to continue taking that "day at a time" approach, trusting that more answers would reveal themselves as time went on. I already had a trip booked to surf in Costa Rica, so six weeks later, I found myself sitting by a salt water pool, overlooking lush greenery, and beyond that, the Pacific Ocean.

Out of nowhere, a dark, ugly cloud of pain overtook me. Suddenly the children splashing in the pool irritated me, and a van full of yogis, eager to start their retreat, nauseated me. Despite the fact that my body was in utopian-level conditions, I still wanted to crawl out of my skin.

At that moment, I realized that there were certain pains originating from inside me. No matter how much effort I put into changing my outside circumstances, I wouldn't achieve any lasting relief unless I addressed the internal disturbances. I could either turn and face them, or spend the rest of my life running. That's the funny thing about The Universe: She's patient.

CHAPTER 6

YOUR "W" IS YOUR WORK…HOWEVER YOU DEFINE IT

———

The concept of "Fake it 'til you make it" always rubbed me the wrong way. After all, wasn't that how I'd gotten myself into this mess? By pretending to be someone or something that I wasn't?!

The suggestion to "Act as if" was doled out pretty frequently in recovery circles, as was "Take what you like and leave the rest." My little (yet extremely loud!) ego made sure suggestions to "Act as if" were promptly assigned to the "things-we're-leaving-behind" category.

Unfortunately, I also happened to be a bundle of raw nerve endings, skittish, and constantly petrified. It wasn't that I needed my liquid courage to walk through fear before—many of my fears were work related and I never drank on the job. However, I frequently used the promise of a drink after work to prod myself into doing whatever petrified me.

Without that carrot, I begrudgingly considered alternative approaches—one of which included "Acting as if."

NOT WHAT I ORDERED—BUT EXACTLY WHAT I'D ASKED FOR

My first morning back in the office (at the tech startup) after my transformational experience at Camp Grounded began the same way I'd started almost every day in sobriety: my usual mindfulness practice (at the time, a mix of reading, meditation, and prayer).

Determined to retain my Gold Dust self when I reentered the real world, I looked for little ways to remind myself throughout the day to connect with who I am at my core. As usual, I stopped at Starbucks for breakfast on my way into work: A reward for making it to an early morning yoga class. (To this day, I continue to use nonalcoholic carrots whenever necessary.) Since this was prior to the days of mobile ordering, it meant that every morning a barista asked me my name and assigned it to my order.

"Venti iced coffee unsweetened with a splash of soy…," the barista confirmed as she marked up the side of the cup with secret Starbucks hieroglyphics. "What's your name?"

"Gold Dust," I answered.

Her marker stopped.

"Gold Dust?" she asked, looking me in the eye.

"Yeah," I stammered, "She's my alter ego. I've got a big day today and—"

"Oh, I get it. Like when Beyoncé channels Sasha Fierce."

She grinned while she finished scribbling out GOLD DUST on the side of the cup.

"Yes! Exactly!" I said, relieved.

While I waited for my drink to be made, I felt a little jolt of inspiration: That seemed exactly like the sort of thing Gold Dust would do.

Making this minute, yet public display of authenticity demanded vulnerability in front of colleagues, work acquaintances, and strangers—relationships where I had little to no ability to assess potential threats to my social safety.

On the other hand, the stakes were pretty low: At worst someone could question my judgment or sanity. I had enough confidence in my own professional and personal reputation that I was willing to risk a dip in my imaginary favorability polls for an additional moment or two in the day where I got to relive the freedom that I felt at Camp Grounded.

I may have finished my risk assessment, but my Inner Critic— Eunice—was just getting warmed up.

MEET EUNICE, MY INNER CRITIC

I didn't even know I had an Inner Critic until I'd had a few years of mindfulness practice under my belt. Not because she holds back with her scathing commentary, or that she speaks in hushed tones: my Inner Critic has narrated my entire life through her judgmental lens. As I go throughout my day, she delivers particularly harsh play-by-play coverage of my experience interacting with the world. Until I knew better, I accepted her broadcast as truth.

In her book *Bird by Bird: Some Instructions on Writing and Life*, Anne Lamott calls this endless chatter radio station KFKD, or K-Fucked:

If you are not careful, station KFKD will play in your head twenty-four hours a day, nonstop, in stereo. Out of the right speaker in your inner ear will come the endless stream of self-aggrandizement, the recitation of one's specialness, of how much more open and gifted and brilliant and knowing and humble one is. Out of the left speaker will be the rap songs of self-loathing, the lists of all the things one doesn't do well, of all the mistakes one has made today and over an entire lifetime, the assertion that everything one touches turns to shit, that one doesn't do relationships well, that one is in every way a fraud, incapable of selfless love, that one has no talent or insight, and on and on and on. [56]

Comforted by the fact that I wasn't the only one trying to function with this madness blaring in the background, I was equally relieved to learn that I could also turn down the volume on her mic.

The Inner Critic's voice is part of the "Self-Zoo of Self Defense Mechanisms" Tesser et al., described in their research related

---

56   Anne Lamott, Bird by Bird: Some Instructions on Writing and Life, (New York: Anchor Books, 1995), 116.

to quieting the ego. [57] It gave our ancestors an evolutionary advantage, helping to label saber tooth tigers as predators, and react accordingly. (I'm assuming the Cro-Magnon version of me would have opted to run, but given my abiding love for felines, I might have run toward the tiger instead of away from it.)

Once I realized that my Inner Critic's voice wasn't actually mine, I found it helpful to further separate her by naming her Eunice and giving her characteristics that seemed to fit her dismal personality and outlook.

If you're curious, Eunice has smoked her entire life, and prefers Virginia Slims. She wears ill-fitting polyester blouses and shoes that look sensible, but are actually a half-size too small, opting to sacrifice both fashion and comfort. She delivers her broadcast using the pair of "cheaters" that hang from a chain around her neck the remainder of the day.

While I waited for the barista making my drink to call out "Gold Dust," Eunice peered at me over the tops of her glasses. Her eyes narrowed further, and she scowled for a moment. Then she launched into her diatribe, which I did my best to let go in one ear and out the other. As she rattled off her litany of concerns, I assumed full risk for the following:

Yes, I was a thirty-four-year-old woman asking my barista to help me actualize a more empowered version of myself by writing my alter ego's name on my cup.

---

57 Abraham et al., "Confluence of Self-Esteem Regulation Mechanisms: On Integrating the Self-Zoo," *Personality and Social Psychology Bulletin*, 26 no. 12 (November 2000): 1476–1489.

Yes, I'd be walking into an office building, directly across from the Sears Tower. (Eunice would like to point out that it's not the Sears Tower anymore—they changed the building's name to "Willis Tower" several years ago.)

Yes, I'd be toting that cup around with me from meeting to meeting, explaining my assessment of the multi-million-dollar accounts that were in my portfolio to manage.

Rolling the dice that someone would see the name written on my Starbucks cup didn't logically seem like a gamble, even though my body and brain were a bit on edge. I knew my motivations were aligned with my authentic self versus my own egotism.

I also knew that failing to form a deeper connection with my authentic self carried an even greater risk: continuing to lop off parts of myself would eventually suffocate me.

"I'VE GOT AN ORDER FOR GOLD DUST"

As the barista slid my finished drink across the counter toward me, I knew this was the perfect way to test drive showing up at my workplace with just a tad more authenticity than before I left for Camp Grounded.

YOUR "W" IS HOWEVER YOU DEFINE IT

Since "Work Talk" was off-limits at Camp Grounded, work became a four-letter word which we referred to as "W." Trying to define what constitutes a workplace, for the purposes of this book, quickly became an exercise in futility. First, the nature of work is changing rapidly, expanding to include recent phenomena like the gig economy and side hustles. Second, hyper-connectivity removes the physical and time constraints that once kept "the workplace" contained within the walls of a brick and mortar building and the daily hours of operation. Third, just because the work is unpaid, doesn't mean it's not work.

To remain within the scope of this book, I'm not able to delve into this issue as deeply as I'd like; however, I would be remiss not to take this opportunity to state what should be obvious, but isn't—especially in America: Not all labor is paid.

If one (or more) human beings depend on your care for some portion of the day, that is most certainly work! This is true for adults taking care of children, as well as adults caring for other adults who need assistance with activities of daily living (ADLs).

You may or may not have an arrangement about this division of labor, but without putting too fine a point on it, if you don't have the option to stay in bed and do whatever you fancy, then it counts as labor. It doesn't matter whether the check paying to keep a roof over your head and food on your plate is made out to you. Put another way, if you were (heaven forbid) hit by a bus, would alternate arrangements need to be made for the care of one or more people? Okay then, it's work.

Most importantly, the mindsets and tools I explain in this book are drawn from universal principles. These will apply anywhere you want to practice showing up as a more authentic version of yourself. That truly is your work—your "W."

As you read this book, I encourage you to apply these tools and mind-sets to the specific situations in your own "W"—however you define it—whenever you need to tap into your own Gold Dust.

CAREER VERSUS JOB VERSUS VOCATION

When I initially began my research for this book, I tried to group findings according to whether they applied to one of three main concepts of "work":

- One's job
- One's career path (including decisions about pursuing additional education)
- One's calling or purpose in life (i.e. a vocation)

Inevitably, the deeper I dove into the personal stories shared with me, the more the lines between these distinctions began to blur. At the end of the day, whether someone's experience showing up as their authentic self at their current job, or in their career, or with respect to what they understand as their calling makes no difference: They are all valid perspectives to use when applying these mindsets and tools to your own life.

Rather than be overly prescriptive in how to categorize the lessons and stories I share here, I've arranged them by theme. Regardless of how you define your "W" or the context in which you view it, my hope is that you'll see the Gold Dust evident in these stories and feel inspired to let your own nature shine through even more.

HR SHOULD DO SOMETHING ABOUT THAT

While I briefly touch on management's role in creating work cultures that encourage authenticity and diversity of thought, I only do so from people whose "W" includes managing people, and their stories exemplify how they model authenticity and vulnerability within the purview of their own "W."

When I first began learning about mindfulness in 2010, I'd partnered with several colleagues in the realm of patient safety to publish a paper on mindfulness and its application in health care. As is the case with group projects—especially those where the participants are spread out across several countries, and where a majority of the participants worked in industry rather than academic settings where the expectation is to "publish or perish"—we performed a cursory review of the literature and held several conference calls, but never quite got the momentum required to sustain our efforts and actually get it published.

Just ten years later, I'm astounded by the amount of research that's been published on various aspects of mindfulness in academic journals. Similarly, topics like mindfulness, wellness, and the interconnected nature of the mind and body are no longer viewed as "new age" or "fringe": They're not only mainstream, products and services are now positioning themselves in ways that claim to align or support the value of mindfulness and its applications.

I deliberately chose not to make the business case for mindfulness in the workplace for two main reasons:

First, marketing departments have already produced this work, using far more sophisticated methods than I could. Their job is to convince investors to financially back their proposed method for training, enabling, or tracking mindfulness practices, that will eventually lead to the promised outcomes—and the projected financial benefits associated with those outcomes. As a rule, I support anything done in the service of wellness promotion. My philosophy is that, provided there's sufficient rigor behind their statistical analysis, I'm agnostic to the profit motive of these companies.

Second, I'm interested in helping people change—and this occurs at the individual level. I, personally, have wasted far too much time and energy trying to change things I couldn't: people, workplaces, institutions. Not only is this a fool's errand—it diverts energy for implementing changes I need to make in my own life.

I support structural change, and do my part when it comes to voting (at the ballot box and with my wallet) for people and companies who represent values consistent with my beliefs, but I've found it to be most helpful for me to "keep my eyes on my own paper" and focus my energy on continuing to show up to all areas of my life as my most authentic Gold Dust self.

Throughout the process of writing this book, one of my (numerous) fears was that I would sound self-righteous or as though I were proselytizing—both of which are postures my ego finds especially appealing. I hope my own mindfulness work, as well as my amazing editors' skills, have saved these pages from wording that seemed too heavy handed.

"I NEVER WANT YOU TO FEEL HORRIBLE FOR BEING A HUMAN BEING"

I never need to know you'll be back online after dinner.

I never need to know why you chose to watch season one of "Arrested Development" (for the fourth time) on your flight to L.A. instead of answering emails.

I never need to know you'll be in late because of a dentist appointment. Or that you're leaving early for your kid's soccer game.

I never need to know why you can't travel on a Sunday.

I never need to know why you don't want to have dinner with me when I'm in your town on a Tuesday night.

I never need to know that you're working from home today because you simply need the silence.

I deeply resent how we've infantilized the workplace. How we feel we have to apologize for having lives. That we don't trust adults to make the right decisions. How constant connectivity/availability (or even the perception of it) has become a valued skill.

I'm equally grateful for the trust/respect my peers, bosses, and teams show me every day.

Years ago, a very senior colleague reacted with incredulity that I couldn't fly on twelve hours' notice because I had my kids that night (and I'm a single dad. edit: divorced). I didn't feel the least bit guilty, which I could tell really bothered said colleague. But it still felt horrible.

I never want you to feel horrible for being a human being.

—IAN SOHN VIA LINKEDIN [58]

WHEN AUTHENTICITY GOES VIRAL

When reflecting on the pivotal moments in his career, Ian Sohn readily admits that his "road less traveled" moment—getting an MBA from NYU's Stern School of Business—is both mundane and evidence of privilege. However, the empathy displayed in his LinkedIn post imploring employees to stop apologizing for being human was extraordinary.

The post went viral, receiving national media attention. Here was someone in a position of power reassuring his employees that the trust and respect was mutual. At the time he wrote his LinkedIn post, Sohn was the CEO of an advertising agency, responsible for nearly 300 employees across four offices.

Clearly, Sohn's words struck a chord. No company's mission statement, vision, or values would be complete

---

58   Ian Sohn, LinkedIn post, Accessed on July 4, 2019.

without some nod to the humans required to bring those words to life. Yet, the expectations of just how much humanity can be tolerated as one is toiling in service of those goals vary widely, with the view of the person to whom one reports carrying the most weight. (As I write this, I feel my own self-righteousness beginning to percolate, right below my sternum.) Setting aside the larger questions this raises around leadership, management, and organizational behavior, I'd like to redirect our focus back to Sohn himself, to explore the ways he ended up being a channel for the message so many of us needed to hear.

Let's circle back to that seemingly ubiquitous MBA: In the world of advertising, an MBA is quite rare. Of the thousands of people that Sohn has met throughout the course of his career, only a handful have an MBA.

Sohn's career in marketing began on the client side, and while living in New York, he earned his graduate degree while working full-time. Unlike the majority of his peers at NYU, who were preparing for careers in finance, Sohn knew he wanted to remain in this field. After ten years on the client side, he switched to the agency side, where he's now been for fourteen years. Though not a prerequisite to be in a leadership position like his, Sohn acknowledges situations where his degree afforded him additional trust from certain clients. More importantly, he recognizes that it opened particular doors for him personally, that led him to where he is today.

"You would be hard-pressed to find somebody running an ad agency who has an MBA...but what I've realized over the years, and can draw a clear line to, is the fact that without it, I, Ian, wouldn't be where I am today. If I hadn't, I wouldn't have gotten my first job out of graduate school, and if I hadn't gotten that job, I wouldn't have gotten my next job, and so on..."

I share similar feelings about my own experience with getting a graduate degree. It's not that the degree itself made me suddenly more capable—it's that the process of attaining it required me to learn how to think and function in new ways. While my particular degree was more common at this level in my field than was Ian's, it also was not a prerequisite and my career progression was similar. Once again, I'm reminded of the Steve Jobs refrain, "You can't connect the dots going forward, you can only connect them looking backward." [59]

More importantly, watching his educational and work experiences line up to support his path to his current role, Sohn explained the gratitude he had for all the leaders he had worked for along the way, both good and bad:

"I have been incredibly blessed to work for people who have been eccentric, and insane, and emotional, and resilient, and compassionate, and clever, and intelligent. And in some cases, also really horrible people....(T)he leader that I am today is nothing more than a composite of all of those people with my own spin put on it."

59   Steve Jobs, Stanford Commencement Address, Stanford.edu, June 14, 2005. Accessed December 26, 2019.

Everyone encouraged by the authenticity in his LinkedIn post benefits from the ripple effect of Sohn's resilience. The next time I find my work involving a person I deem "horrible," I hope to have the presence of mind to remember that the possibility exists for me to transform less than ideal circumstances into management gold.

PART 3

WHAT WOULD GOLD DUST DO?

CHAPTER 7

FOLLOW YOUR BLISS

———

When I stopped living life by my brain power and sheer force of will, and started approaching life from the perspective of one node of a much larger whole (a speck of gold dust amongst other specks of gold dust, if you will), I found myself suddenly questioning other big ticket items in life: Whether or not I actually wanted to get married again, or have children, or stay in the same career. Since I'd already had experience reinventing myself with a career change prior to recovery, making another switch seemed plausible. My bigger concern was, and still is, whether or not I was trying to treat a symptom instead of addressing the root cause.

I'll share some of the most inspiring people and stories I've gathered about people who exude authenticity in their work. Some seem to have followed their bliss (à la Joseph Campbell) directly into a career, others have integrated their calling into their vocation, while still others have taken a leap in a new direction, when they've either felt led (or been dragged) into a new arena. Regardless of the path these particular individuals chose, I've found inspiration and encouragement by learning about their experience—especially as it pertains to making career decisions from my most authentic self.

FOLLOW YOUR BLISS—EVEN WHEN IT'S AT ODDS WITH YOUR TRIBE

Sitting on the beach with the other girls, watching the guys surf, Andreina "Andre" Poletti longed to be out there surfing herself.

Having grown up in Costa Rica, a surfer's paradise, Andre's call to adventure made perfect sense; yet, her mother was careful to keep her daughter focused on other goals, including those involving Andre's future. Recognizing her daughter's drive and wanting her to realize her full potential, Andre's mother stressed the importance of getting a college education. As Andre was completing her final year of high school, getting a degree in hotel management and returning to run the family business seemed like a sensible plan, at least from her parents' perspective.

Determined to become a surfer, Andre bought her first surfboard that summer: a yellow 6'0" short board. Shorter boards are designed for performance. The less volume a board has, the harder it is to stay balanced enough to stand up on. Beginners often start with longboards, around ten to twelve feet, and occasionally with a semi-padded top. Trying to learn on a board with less volume only made Andre's challenge that much harder.

She charged into the ocean anyway. Her stomach positioned in the middle of the freshly waxed board, she paddled *out the back*—the place in the water past the impact zone, where the waves are breaking. In this respect, her short board's lighter volume made it easier to dive underneath the breaking wave ("duck dive") like she'd seen the more experienced surfers do. After making it beyond the impact zone, she paddled around on her board like the other surfers. She watched their body language and movements, as they sat upright on their boards, backs toward the shore, facing the horizon, eyes squinting as they surveyed the surface of the water.

Reading the waves is as mysterious as it is frustrating: the moment one learns to identify an aspect signifying a "good" (i.e. rideable) wave, various other skills must also come into play: quickly turning around, then paddling to the spot a surfer needs to be to get enough of a runway to get the requisite paddles in to be going fast enough to catch the wave. Then there's the mechanics of popping up on the board, with the feet, hips, hands, and head in the proper position. If you manage to successfully check all those boxes, your next feat is to sense yourself beginning to fall and override your natural instinct to lean back. If you can keep your weight centered on the board, you'll remain upright as you drop onto the open face of the wave. Like a skateboarder pausing briefly at the edge before sliding down onto the sloping wall of an empty pool, you'll effortlessly trace a path that doesn't seem like it should be traversable.

With so many critical items on the execution checklist, surfing's learning curve is a steep one. Andre ended up paddling around on her board, as though she were auditioning for the role of surfer waiting for her wave, and eventually washing back up on shore, looking like "a drowned rat." Still, she had at least moved from the safety of her previous post: sitting on shore by the other girls.

At the end of summer, she left for her freshman year of college. Boston's distance and cold temperatures were constant reminders that she was no longer in San Jose. She begged her mom to let her come home, but managed to finish out her semester. She returned home, enrolling in a college nearby.

On weekends, she'd return to the beach, hellbent on learning to surf. These trips mimicked the same paddling, effort, and dashed hopes as her first attempt, with each session ending with her on shore, exhausted, and watching others surf with ease. After struggling to teach herself what to do, she would end up having complete meltdowns on the shore. Even with expert instruction, surfing is a frustrating pursuit, with hours of hard work seemingly resulting in little to no progress. Then suddenly, all the pieces click into place, and voilà! You're riding!

The tenacity required to continue getting pummeled by the waves, day after day, in the hopes of catching a wave can't be overstated; yet, Andre's mother didn't see it that way. Even though Andre had been taking classes in San Jose, her mother began pressuring Andre to go back and finish what she had started with her education in the United States.

Looking back, Andre notes that her mother's persistence had nothing to do with the quality of education offered in one country versus the other. Andre's mother wanted her daughter to expand her horizons, in addition to seeing a challenging goal through to its completion.

Andre agreed, but only under two conditions: She would transfer to a school someplace where there was sun, and she'd major in psychology. Her mother countered with a double major in psychology and business, and before long, Andre landed in Miami.

Miami may be sunny, but it's not known for its waves. Still, Andre brought her board with her to the states. Picking her board up from oversize baggage claim, she walked around the airport like a professional athlete.

"Can I tell you how cool I felt just traveling with my surfboard? Standing there like I knew what I was doing?!" she recalls. "It was like wearing a medal...'*That's right. I'm a surfer girl.*'"

Taking the classes needed to finish her degree didn't leave Andre any time for surfing, except one trip to Fort Lauderdale with a friend who also happened to surf. That trip ended up being a repeat of the same frustrating attempts back in Costa Rica: paddling around the whole time, but never getting up on a wave. Except for that trip, her surfboard remained in the corner of her room. It wasn't just decoration though—it was also inspiration.

She graduated, having done what her parents wanted her to do: Get an education. When she returned to Costa Rica, she decided it was time for her to do what *she* wanted to do, which included moving to the beach.

"Why?" Her mother demanded.

"Because I want to learn how to surf," Andre explained.

"Excuse me?! You just got your education! You are a business and a psychology major! Now you are supposed to get a job."

Her mother's voice took a more serious tone, "If you do that, you're on your own. We're not going to help you at all."

Undeterred, Andre moved to the beach. Determined to learn how to surf, she spent her days in the ocean and got a job waiting tables at night. She still had her yellow short board, but no one to teach her what to do.

It took a long time, but eventually she did it.

Andre isn't the only benefactor of her hard-won surfing skills: She taught me how to surf (and numerous others) as well. After one particularly frustrating session in the ocean, I had a meltdown of my own. Despite paddling with all my might, I couldn't seem to get past the impact zone. My arms were as useless as two plastic sacks of jam.

I plopped down in the sand, ripped the Velcro securing the leash around my ankle, and began sobbing. My Inner Critic—who had been running her negative mouth the entire trip—had all sorts of things to say, including that this was why people didn't take up surfing in their mid-thirties and that I'd never be able to ride a wave—neither of which turned out to be true.

Andre joined me on the shore. I looked up, my face covered in a mixture of salt water, tears, and snot. She began to share her own frustrating experiences learning how to surf.

It never occurred to me that someone who made surfing look so effortless had ever struggled. Years later, I still remember the hope and encouragement I gleaned from her that day on the beach. She explained that progress in surfing, like most things in life, wasn't linear. And that I'd have sessions that were good, along with sessions that weren't so good—but that the point was to keep at it because the waves would continue to keep coming, always and forever, just like Mother Ocean.

Years later, after I'd made several return trips to Costa Rica and spent three months surfing around the coast of South Africa and Mozambique, I knew I wanted to capture the gifts I received from Andre's strength as well as her own struggle. The same inner voice that kept calling her to surf resonates within me too.

She explains, "I'm so glad that I heard my instinct. All I wanted to do was learn how to surf. Little did I know that this was going to take me not only to the best version of me. But also, to be able to sustain myself and be happy."

FOLLOW YOUR BLISS...EVEN IF IT YOU HAVE TO DO IT SCARED

Bob Conlin had achieved more success in his healthcare career than colleagues twice his age: He had an MBA, an impressive title and the salary to match. Having worked as a registered nurse in the early years of his career, Bob gained valuable experience that informed his decision-making and earned him the respect of his colleagues and staff.

Self-awareness is one of many factors contributing to Bob's success. He's also quick to acknowledge how critical his support system, which includes relationship-based coaching, is to helping push him beyond his perceived limitations.

Bob explains, "Not that it's wrong or bad—but by nature, I'm not going to push my boundaries [to the same extent that] I would if I have literally, a whole team of people around me, reminding me of what's possible, reminding me of what I want—or said I wanted—in life...reminding me of who I am."

Relationship-based coaching made such a profound effect on his life, Bob completed the training and certification to become a coach himself. Helping his clients transform their lives continues to be a deeply gratifying part of his life.

Bob's healthcare management career continued to grow as well; yet, he found himself returning home from work feeling physically exhausted and emotionally depleted. His corporate job provided him security: it gave him a respectable identity and financial stability. Yet, when he reflected on his gifts, and the impact he wanted to make on the planet, he knew his current position was not allowing him to do that. Increasingly, he found himself at the end of each day asking, "Is this it?"

After wrestling with these questions, Bob eventually reached his decision point: Continue with the status quo or leave the security of corporate America and pour his time, energy, and resources into his coaching practice.

Like any natural progression, Bob's journey consisted of tiny leaps of faith along the way: Preparation for this gigantic leap unfolding over several years. He began by recruiting additional support for his new life. This included shoring up identified gaps physically, emotionally, and spiritually, so that he was fully resourced to support this "new normal." He strengthened these areas through recommitting to nutrition and exercise; enlisting the help of coaches and therapists; and developing the daily rituals that connected him to his internal wisdom and purpose.

Bob acknowledges the mental trap of waiting for the absence of fear to indicate that he was headed in the right direction. Bob credits having effective coaches in his life kept him accountable when the clamors of daily life competed for his attention, drawing him away from his true desires. Bob explains,

"I have these people constantly, consistently reminding me, 'Hey, this is what you want...and this is what you're putting in the way every day to not have it.' And, ultimately, I can sum it down to one thing. It's fear."

When he realized that using the "absence of fear" as an indicator that the timing was right might permanently delay his jump, he began to ask a new question, "Could I feel the fear and jump anyway?"

He continued to move forward with his plans, feeling the fear and yet taking the steps to leave the security of corporate America anyway. The voices of fear weren't just coming from inside, though: People in Bob's life felt compelled to voice their own concerns about his decision, and tried to persuade him from what they viewed to be a tragic mistake. Though he had the support of his wife, Shona Moeller, and other key figures in his life, pleas for him to reconsider came pouring in.

Bob says, "People went out of their way...to tell me what a big mistake I was making."

A range of people, from friends he hadn't spoken to in months to his mother-in-law, tried to reason him out of leaving his job. He recalls the well-intended, but hurtful "interventions" from a compassionate stance. He realized their projections of fear were their own, and that they were simply trying to show their love for him, and advocate for his happiness, even though their words did more harm than good.

"I finally realized that, they were just loving me and trying to protect me," he said.

He shared his appreciation for others' well-intended concerns, and acknowledged that, to some extent, he shared those same concerns. Yet his fear of looking back with regret outweighed any fear he had of failure.

Bob recalls his standard response to these outreach attempts:

"I'd say, 'Hey, I hear you. I'm scared too...but if I don't do this, I'm going to spend the rest of my life wishing I had. Worst case scenario, I fail. If I fail, I can go back to health care, or create something different, whatever that is.'"

Bob's own mother wasn't entirely sold on his plan either. He remembers the moment she reached a turning point. Halfway through a conversation they'd already had numerous times, she paused and asked him to follow the advice he'd give a client facing the same decision.

Bob already knew he had to follow through on his dream. At that moment, his mother knew he had to take that path as well.

FOLLOW YOUR BLISS...IF IGNORING
IT WOULD LEAVE YOU WITH REGRET

When customers ask Derrick Tung how he went from a career in hospital administration to owning a pizza joint, he tells them it was a midlife crisis, but Derrick's love for sharing pizza with the ones he loves goes back to the second grade.

For children growing up in the 80's, the connection between pizza and reading is an easy one to make: Pizza Hut's "Book It!" program awarded children who hit their monthly reading goals with a coupon for a free personal pan pizza. Derrick's parents immigrated to the U.S. with little money, so luxuries like dining out were a rarity. Derrick saved up his free pizza coupons and every few months, he'd take his family out for pizza.

After achieving early success in his career as a hospital administrator, Derrick began channeling his passions back into pizza, building his own mobile wood-fired pizza oven and selling his creations at fairs and farmer's markets. During his time as a hybrid entrepreneur (an entrepreneur also working a full-time job) he continued developing his culinary skills and researching the market.

Tung also looked for people who could potentially mentor him, should he continue to follow his entrepreneurial dreams. Mentors had already helped him achieve success in the corporate world, and he knew pursuing an even riskier path would require the guidance of someone with more experience. He was especially interested in learning from someone who had a similar background, and could understand his perspective. Derrick wanted a mentor who had not grown up in the restaurant industry, as well as someone who understood the inherent risks in making a big career transition. He also wanted to learn from someone who, like himself, did not belong to the small contingent of diehard Italians who believe heritage is a necessary ingredient for superior pizza.

Derrick formed connections with several potential mentors, but his relationship with Paulie Gee flourished, and they cemented the bond with Derrick opening up the Chicago franchise location with Paulie Gee's name on it.

Reflecting back on his decision-making process, Derrick recalls the conversations he had with his wife, Cathy (also an entrepreneur). When Paulie approached him with the opportunity, Derrick and Cathy spent three nights reviewing the pros and cons, and finally settled the matter by asking the question: If we didn't take this opportunity, would we regret it?

When the answer was *yes*, they knew they had to give it a try.

YOU WILL ENCOUNTER ADDITIONAL DECISION POINTS ALONG THE WAY

Despite the blood, sweat, and tears required to open his pizzeria, unforeseen challenges made the early days a struggle. Opening night turned into an opening nightmare: Backed up plumbing flooded the restaurant and they had to vacate the space. Six months in, the restaurant was in bad shape financially: They were losing money every day and considered cutting their losses and shutting down.

Again, Derrick and Cathy took stock of the situation, and realized that walking away at that point would likely fill them with regret. In addition to securing additional investors, Derrick also took a meticulous eye to how they were operating, identified areas for improvement, and implemented those changes immediately. Gradually, the tides began to turn. And three and a half years in, they are in a far better place, and expect to turn a quarter million profit in 2019.

Success consists of far more than the number at the bottom line, and Derrick's commitment to his staff, as well as his involvement with the Logan Square community, continually demonstrate his decision to operate from a mindset of abundance versus one driven by scarcity and fear. A firm believer in the idea that a high tide raises all boats, Derrick partners with local chefs, small businesses, and restaurants—including other pizza places.

Derrick explains, "You can choose to see them as competition, or as colleagues."

Unless a pizzeria opens next to his with the same offerings: Detroit-style square pizzas or wood-fired Neapolitan-inspired pizzas, his view is that people will gravitate toward the particular style that appeals to them anyway: with ovens fired by wood, gas, or coal and styles influenced by the cities in which they originated in (e.g., New York, Chicago, or Detroit).

"If we've got a two-hour wait, and people are looking for pizza, why not let them know about other places down the street that you believe are making a great pizza as well, and sharing the love?"

FOLLOWING YOUR BLISS EMPOWERS
OTHERS TO FOLLOW THEIRS TOO

Pursuing internal growth reveals many paradoxes, one of which is that operating from my authentic self becomes less and less about me—and more about connecting with other people.

By acknowledging the worth inherent in my own allotment of gold dust, I can recognize the inherent worth of everyone around me. Through my own radical acceptance of myself—both my strengths and my weaknesses—I have more compassion available for those around me, and a greater capacity and willingness to meet them where they are.

CHAPTER 8

THE JUICE IS WORTH THE SQUEEZE

———

BEING YOUR AUTHENTIC SELF
ALLOWS YOU TO EFFECT CHANGE

When I first met Maggie Meiners, I had no idea what kind of person she was or what she did for a living, but I knew I liked her already. I can be shallow. Maggie's sleek platinum hair, glowing complexion, and round brown eyes made her plenty glamorous in my book. Her surface details, which also included an attractive husband, two adorable boys, and a home in Winnetka, an affluent suburb of Chicago, were all the credentials I needed to put her on my short list of ego ideals. (Had I been able to assemble her life from the 1988 JC Penny catalog, I certainly would have.)

Not long into our first conversation, I knew her beauty ran well-beyond surface level. And she had a rebellious streak similar to my own.

Meiners, a fine art photographer and filmmaker, acknowledges that she is a disrupter, but she makes waves as a result of following her authentic self—not from a contrarian disposition.

She notes that living in a conservative community where people are fashionable can also be mundane—especially since she's worked to rid her life of toxicity and drama.

Maggie explains,

"It's a pretty monotonous existence. It's…lovely and Mayberry…So [when she goes] to the grocery store [she asks] 'What can I wear to throw people off a little bit?' Not because I'm looking for attention, but because I need to break up the monotony. It makes it look like I'm going down this path that no one else is, but it all comes from a really authentic place."

Maggie doesn't eschew the privilege that her race and upper middle-class upbringing afforded her—and she doesn't ignore the benefits she could easily take for granted. A fine art photographer and filmmaker, art is her means of working through her inner conflict. Making art allows her to exert an element of control over an inner dialogue that, at times, finds her at odds with the world around her.

"I was totally raised upper middle-class WASP, and while those are all my people, I have this conflict with some of the values and some of the ways issues are addressed. My art is not about controlling the external world. It's really about controlling my inner conflict, and creating a narrative that I can put out there."

Like many Americans, Maggie is bothered by the increasing rhetoric of fear associated with racial and religious communities. Shortly after President Trump's inauguration, an American-born Muslim man spoke at Maggie's church. Both struck by his story—and bothered by the fact that she didn't know anyone from the Muslim faith—she asked the man out for coffee.

During their conversation, she expressed her concerns that Muslims especially seemed to be targeted—and she expressed her desire to help illuminate the blind spots others might unknowingly have, especially if they didn't have a personal connection with someone from the Muslim community. She then asked if he would be willing to help her with a photography project. [60]

The man gathered his friends who agreed to pose for her interpretation of Norman Rockwell's "Freedom of Worship." The original painting showed subtle differences in the way each of the congregants prayed, meant to depict Americans' freedom to express their religious devotion to their own concept of God: for example, a rosary is visible in one parishioner's hands, but not in any others. [61] The phrase "Each according to the dictates of his own conscience" is centered at the top. [62]

In Meiners' rendition, the same phrase now sits atop a group of Muslim worshippers, including a woman wearing a hijab patterned after the American Flag. "I want to expand

---

60 Laura Holson, "Reimagining Norman Rockwell's America," *New York Times*, November 8, 2018.
61 "Freedom of Worship," Totally History (website), Accessed January 25, 2020.
62 Ibid.

dialogue," Maggie said. "The value of art is that it can connect people on all levels." [63]

This willingness to listen and seek to understand another's perspective is critical to art as dialogue versus art as statement. The former is a two-way method of communication; the latter seems only concerned with artist's point of view.

Prior to getting sober, Meiners controlled her world through images. Meiners explains,

"When I first started making art...I was so internally messed up...so chaotic, spiritually, and emotionally, that my pictures were very graphic. [There was] lots of black and white. There was no gray. I couldn't control myself. So, I had to control the world with my camera."

I associate the phrase "comfort the afflicted and afflict the comfortable" with Ms. Meiners' experience of the world and her art. Journalist and humorist Finley Peter Dunne is credited with giving us this phrase in reference to the power and responsibility of journalism. In one of his columns for the *Chicago Evening Post* in 1893, Dunne gave us this concept via his fictional character Mr. Dooley, a nineteenth century barkeep, as a mouthpiece. [64] Dunne spoke through a fictional character in the same way Meiners speaks through her camera lens. The evolution of Ms. Meiners' art, from one of

---

63   Laura Holson, "Reimagining Norman Rockwell's America," *New York Times*, November 8, 2018.

64   David Shedden, "Today in Media History: Mr. Dooley: 'The job of the newspaper is to comfort the afflicted and afflict the comfortable,'" *Poynter*, October 7, 2014.

controlling the world via her camera lens to channeling her internal conflict into a clear voice that she puts out there for the purpose of creating dialogue, mirrors the same journalistic higher purpose shared by Dunne's character.

WE ARE ALL CREATORS

"As a maker, I have to make things in order to know my world. I think that's what led me to this road less traveled, if you will. I'm so in tune with the energy that surrounds me. And I'm so in tune to my physical reaction to stimulus, and sound and color and joy and sorrow and other people's energy. It really ignites me to create the world I want to see."

Maggie recounts how this impulse manifested itself during her recent trip to Iceland. Admittedly, the timing of her visit wasn't ideal: Due to the changing seasons, Iceland's vistas— though beautiful—were draped in muted tones of gray and brown. She found herself photographing the vast landscapes all day long, then returning to her hotel and adding psychedelic flourishes to the day's images.

Given Ms. Meiners' penchant for bringing comfort to the afflicted and afflicting the comfortable, this concept of photoshopping landscapes struck me as inconsistent. I pried deeper.

To be clear, Meiners is not the type of person who alters photographs to create a fantasy world where she can escape from reality.

Alarmed by the climate crisis, Maggie is a conscious consumer. She also prioritizes spending time in nature to fill her spiritual well. Her trip to Iceland was meant to reenergize her spiritual connection, yet the natural world surrounding her was literally beige. With that visual image as a metaphor for the ailing health of our planet, she relied on her creativity to revive her subject matter—and her spirits.

"I'm really connected to the earth, spiritually, but it wasn't bringing me any joy. So, I had to create that joy in my images."

DON'T LET FEAR STOP YOU FROM USING YOUR VOICE

On her podcast, *Magic Lessons with Elizabeth Gilbert,* the author of *Eat, Pray, Love,* and *Big Magic: Creative Living Beyond Fear,* interviews ordinary people struggling with creative blocks. She offers insight from her own experience to encourage fledgling artists of all types to move beyond the fears that limit them. Gilbert often enlists the help of other noteworthy authors, artists, and performers within her own network to seek additional guidance on behalf of her callers. She ends each episode by checking in on the artists several weeks after their initial conversation to for a progress report.

While washing dishes one day, I heard the episode in which spoken-word poet, Hope Hill, discusses her struggles to share poetry with wider audiences. [65] She's afraid of exposing herself and her art in an arena where she might receive negative feedback—like poetry contests or publications. [66] Elizabeth

---

65 Elizabeth Gilbert and Martha Beck, "Episode 208: Leap Into the Fire," September 16, 2016, Magic Lessons with Elizabeth Gilbert, podcast, 1:19:28.

66 Ibid.

Gilbert gently reminds her that rejection is part of the privilege of having a public voice. [67]

As one of her assignments, Gilbert asks Hill to write herself a letter from her great grandmother, talking about what life was like without being able to advocate for herself publicly. [68]

The gravity of that assignment was so powerful, I stopped mid-dish.

My voice is the most public of all the women in my own lineage. And I have the benefit of white privilege.

Hope Hill was not only the first in her family to have this public voice—she was only a few generations removed from ancestors *who had been enslaved.*

Next, Gilbert reached out to author (and Oprah's life coach) Martha Beck, for additional insight. Beck acknowledges the reality that pain is a part of the human experience, and that avoidance of pain only leads to additional suffering, like addiction and artistic suffocation. While we can't avoid pain, we can learn how to be resilient. She maintains the only reason for creativity is to experience what the human soul feels like, and in that vulnerable and heart-broken state, to learn how to access grace. [69]

---

67 Ibid.

68 Ibid.

69 Elizabeth Gilbert and Martha Beck, "Episode 208: Leap Into the Fire," September 16, 2016, Magic Lessons with Elizabeth Gilbert, podcast, 1:19:28.

"There on the bathroom floor, what you open to is not other people's advice about art, it is your own voice. The voice, as Mary Oliver says, 'that you slowly began to recognize as your own.' And [that voice] always does one thing. It offers you kindness." [70]

Beck illustrates her point using a story from Gilbert's own book *Eat, Pray, Love*. Having reached her breaking point, Liz Gilbert is sobbing on her bathroom floor.

Beck explains,

"That's what happened to you, right? [The voice said], 'Go back to bed, Liz.'" [71]

Beck describes that moment as turning unbearable suffering into "just barely tolerable." That switch is what set off the whole expansion of that void that Gilbert chronicled in her book—and that continues to expand today. [72] Beck sums it up perfectly:

"All art and creativity must be (about the expansion of that void) because you're going to serve one of two things: you're going to serve ego or you're going to serve love." [73]

---

70   Ibid.
71   Ibid.
72   Elizabeth Gilbert and Martha Beck, "Episode 208: Leap Into the Fire," September 16, 2016, Magic Lessons with Elizabeth Gilbert, podcast, 1:19:28.
73   Ibid.

CHAPTER 9

FINDING THE BALANCE

---

*"God turns you from one feeling to another
and teaches by means of opposites so that
you will have two wings to fly, not one"*

—RUMI [74]

I prefer to follow my inner compass rather than following a strict set of rules to the letter; yet, ambiguity can be equally overwhelming. After all, the brain helping me decide my next move is the same brain that convinced me having another drink was a good idea—even though I had plenty of evidence to the contrary. It was easier to see how my judgment would be impaired after I'd already ingested some alcohol, but what about the countless times I'd sworn off alcohol and still managed to convince myself "this time will be different" while I was stone cold sober?!

---

74 Goodreads (website), "The Essential Rumi," (Accessed October 11, 2019). https://www.goodreads.com/work/quotes/965212-essential-rumi.

In addition to accepting that my body does not process alcohol in the same way a nonalcoholic does, I also had to accept that my thinking is equally flawed. Once I ingest alcohol, I can't control how much I subsequently consume. And I have a mind obsessed with getting the relief I once found in alcohol, even though I know the consequences of taking another drink would be devastating.

I've heard it said that an alcoholic's brain wants the alcoholic dead, but will settle for miserable. When I slack off on my spiritual work (my mindfulness practices in addition to all the suggested components of twelve-step recovery) it doesn't take long before the obsessive thoughts fire up again. I can count on one hand the number of times they've specifically involved a desire for alcohol, but I am the MacGyver of vices: I can make an addiction out of anything.

This brings me to what I consider to be black belt mindfulness work: How do I know if the voice I hear is my authentic self? Or is it just my ego doing its "authentic self" impersonation?

At first, I didn't know. I did the best I could, but made a number of mistakes.

Like Bambi on ice, I tried my best to stay upright while walking over the frozen pond. In the Disney classic, the little fawn gingerly takes a few steps onto the slippery surface. Suddenly, his hooves slide out from under him and he lands on his belly, legs splayed out in all directions.

CAN'T TELL IF YOU'RE HEARING YOUR EGO OR YOUR AUTHENTIC SELF? TRY THESE OPTIONS:

PAUSE

If a decision is not necessary at the moment, I wait until I get more clarity. Sometimes the best action I can take is to do nothing. As someone who is action-oriented, this was excruciating to put into practice. Gradually, I began to see that my impulse to do something was often a reactionary response after experiencing a triggering situation. The more I healed, the less my nervous system sent warning signals to my body to leap into action.

Since I was no longer rushing in to save the day, I was amazed at how other people became willing to take their turn at superhero duty. I was equally shocked to see how many "emergency" situations actually turned out to be false alarms. By learning to hang back a bit, I found I had more energy in the tank for the type of work I enjoyed doing: Creative work requiring sustained periods of intense focus. I also reduced any unnecessary confusion and drama resulting from my feverish attempts to solve a problem that didn't actually exist.

If a decision must be made, I do my best then let it go. With continued practice—both in quieting my ego and in learning to listen to and trust my inner compass—discernment between the two becomes easier.

ELIMINATE THE OPTIONS YOU KNOW TO BE INCORRECT

Even if I'm not clear about what the next right action is, I can usually ascertain which actions *not* to take.

Life is course correcting: Even if we end up heading down the second or third best path, we can always turn around. We're still likely to be in better shape than if we'd just picked a path at random.

REMEMBER THE SPECTRUM

My brain likes to think in black and white terms, while real life is comprised of various shades of gray. When I notice my thoughts start to vacillate between one extreme and its opposite, I imagine that they're on a spectrum, and my only job is to find the ideal spot between the two poles, just for this moment.

LET SOMEONE ELSE IN ON IT

Anxiety paralyzes me. Sometimes it operates via "paralysis by analysis" where my brain becomes so obsessed with running through each of the potential scenarios that I'm not only more likely to miss the bigger picture, I can also miss the opportunity entirely.

Conversely, my fear can also disguise itself as procrastination. Unlike the scenario above, I'm eager to push related information out of my brain, as though forgetting about it will make it go away, forever. Eventually, it pops up again, like a mental boomerang with an uncanny sense of timing.

As soon as I recognize I'm getting sucked into either of those mental traps, I've found the best thing I can do is tell someone about it. Verbalizing it, especially with a friend or colleague lightens my mental load. My relationships with personal friends and colleagues can then grow to a deeper level, because we're able to talk about what's really going on in our lives, versus keeping things strictly superficial.

PUT IT BACK INTO PERSPECTIVE

It helps to remind myself I'm just making the best decision I can for today—I'm not setting a hard and fast rule for the rest of eternity. I also find these opportunities to be excellent times to ask The Universe to give me a little nudge in the right direction, via my gut instinct.

OPTIONS WHEN THE STAKES ARE HIGHER

One of the most challenging situations for me to discern between what's ego and what's love is when I'm doing something new—where I have a gut instinct about where I'm heading, but it contradicts the guidance of the person who has more authority or experience.

Depending on the circumstances, I will usually attempt to follow the more experienced person's guidance. If it continues to feel wrong, I reserve the right to try again, this time pursuing my original idea. With these decisions, especially in cases where I don't have enough of a track record with the authority figure or expert to know if I trust them, I use as many of the options outlined above as I can to help me decide the best course of action.

Remembering that occasionally I have to lose a battle to win a war helps, as does asking myself if that's the particular hill I want to die on.

It's interesting to note how common these battle metaphors come up in the workplace. Our perception colors our reality. If feeling like I'm at war is a reoccurring theme, it's useful data. It may signal that I need to change something, either internally or externally, because I prefer to operate from a collaborative, supportive environment, like Camp Grounded, than from one that feels like a battle zone.

VOICING THE MINORITY OPINION

An additional layer of difficulty is added when a decision like the one above is being made in a group setting and my instincts run contrary to the general consensus. Again, I try to pause, ask for an intuitive thought or decision, and trust that the wisdom of the group will lead us to the right outcome.

I reserve my right to voice the minority opinion, and have chosen to voice an unpopular opinion when misguided group-think appeared to be taking over. In those instances where I feel compelled to speak up, I find that during the time I pause and listen to other people, if a collective madness seems to be inhibiting critical thinking skills, I will notice increasing discomfort in my body, and often feel sick to my stomach. That worsening feeling signals to me that it's time to speak up.

Here are three questions I still find helpful when trying to decide to speak now—or forever hold my peace:

- Does it need to be said?
- Does it need to be said by me?
- Does it need to be said by me now?

DON'T COMPROMISE ON YOUR VISION...

In my conversation with gym owner David Sutor, I asked how he approached similar situations. He noticed these gray areas happening more in the areas of his life outside the gym.

"Compromise is gross. It's a watered-down version of what you thought was cool: A business plan, a design for a house, a book, or a relationship...If you have a vision and start compromising on it, now it's not yours, so how can you fully lean into it?"

David and his girlfriend, Nicole, recently completed extensive renovations on a home in Andersonville, one of Chicago's charming and trendy neighborhoods on the north side of the city. Their home is open and modern, with lots of white, natural materials, and a minimalist vibe. Large windows in the front and back of the house flood the open floor plan with natural light. Nicole says they spend a majority of their time at home on the main floor, along with their mastiffs, Charlie and Stan, and it's easy to see why. They had a vision and achieved it—but not without significant pushback from contractors, architects, and inspectors who felt their plans were ill-advised.

I interviewed David at an oversized island in the middle of their kitchen. Four grey upholstered swivel stools line one side of the slab of white marble. While seated, I can look at the white subway tile backsplash and stainless-steel appliances, or swivel slightly to the left and look out onto their large porch and backyard—features any city dweller would want to optimize.

Countless professionals tried to talk them out of it, saying the island was too big for the space, and that it would feel crowded once they'd moved in their furnishings.

"Nicole and I had a vision of how we would sit in our kitchen, and we [felt like saying], 'You don't sit in our kitchen!' From a technical standpoint, yes, you have to make sure your plans are up to code, but we wouldn't compromise on the rest of it," David explains.

Fortunately, David and Nicole stayed true to their vision—and executed it masterfully, completing all the work themselves. When critics viewed the finished result, they were thoroughly impressed.

...EXCEPT WHEN YOU NEED TO COMPROMISE ON YOUR VISION

Shifting to the topic of Crossfit Defined, the gym David opened with his business partner nine years ago, Sutor acknowledges that he often compromises, rather than rigidly sticking to his preferred approach because he's surrounded by talented coaches who bring their own ideas and passion to coaching athletes and designing challenging workouts that are equally grounded in exercise science, leadership, and creativity.

David admits,

"Here's the tough part: I've got a 50/50 business partner, and twelve coaches who are amazing at what they do and have been with us for at least five or six years now...Learning how to flow between all of these alphas has been the hardest thing in the world."

Workplace tension can occasionally seep out in less formal work environments, like gyms and yoga studios. When clients visit an establishment on a regular basis, in addition to developing relationships with the staff, they can also pick up on shifts in energy and atmosphere due to unspoken conflict brewing behind the scenes.

I've trained at Crossfit Defined for two and a half years, and have never experienced a discordant vibe there. On the contrary, my love for this gym, and the people who train there, is a direct result of how open, accepting, and diverse our community is. We're committed to becoming the best versions of ourselves that we can be, and that includes acknowledging and accepting that comparing ourselves to the person working out next to us is not conducive to the sustained growth we're trying to achieve. David credits Crossfit Defined's success, at least in part, to the fact that his coaches are all experts in their respective fields—and that they all have each other's backs.

When it comes to the issue of having to compromise, however, he notes that they all bring their unique strengths, ideas, and perspectives. He admits he is heavily biased toward strength training. (He currently holds five national lifting titles—a fact I only discovered through background research.) [75]

When asked for an example of where he had to quiet his own ego and allow someone else the opportunity to pursue their vision, he responds,

"All the conditioning classes at Defined."

---

75 "The Coaching Team," Defined Strength and Conditioning, accessed January 23, 2020.

Knowing the cult-like popularity of these classes and the coaches who lead them makes his response even more astounding. He explains,

"I couldn't see past my bias, which is obviously the strength component. They wanted to do this stuff—and to me, it was like nails on a chalkboard."

He references his earlier comment about compromise being watered-down and gross, but counters it with the realization that he instinctually hired these coaches in the first place. David says,

"You also have to trust that you hired them to bring the thunder. So, let them bring the thunder. If they fail? Cool. What did we learn?"

David doesn't automatically use the lesson as evidence to support implementing his original idea either. He's pleasantly surprised by the mutual trust and respect that comes with allowing his staff the opportunity to experiment and grow. He shares his current approach on encouraging his staff to take risks:

"Actually, I hope you fail. And I hope you get something out of it. Then I want you to come back in two weeks, and try it again, delivering an even better version of it."

KNOWING WHEN TO FOLLOW GUIDANCE...AND WHEN TO FOLLOW YOUR INNER COMPASS

Earlier, I explained the importance of mentors in shaping Derrick Tung's earlier career in healthcare administration as well as his current entrepreneurial endeavor as the owner of the Paulie Gee's franchise in Chicago. Given Derrick's reputation as a thoughtful and logical business owner, I was correct in my assumption that his assessment of the next right move for the pizzeria often aligned with Paulie Gee, his current mentor, as well.

Selfishly, I hoped he had some advice about how he approached situations where they weren't in agreement, simply because I want to learn how others handle those times when your intuition is at odds with the guidance received from a trusted source. Just like his pizza, Derrick didn't disappoint.

During the first six months it was open, the pizzeria was losing money. They sold wood-fired Neapolitan pizzas—the style that gained Paulie Gee notoriety—and three days a week, they sold Detroit style square pizzas, which are baked in pans, using gas ovens. Derrick was still testing the Chicago market to see how it would react to the Detroit-style offering.

Derrick explains,

"I met with Paulie during that period where we were losing money, and he asked, 'Why are you focusing on Detroit style? Just cut that off until you figure out how to become profitable with what you have.'"

While on its face, Paulie's logic was sound, Derrick had the additional insight of being in his restaurant all week, inter-acting with guests, and hearing how much they liked the

Detroit-style option. He also began getting a lot of press because of the square-shaped pizza's novelty.

"Against his advice, I actually expanded it."

Derrick conducted a trial, bringing on a person to see if they could increase their profitability by offering the Detroit-style pizzas full time.

His risk paid off: the square pizzas now account for 40 percent of his sales.

"It's a gigantic draw....Detroit style is not really widespread in the Chicago market."

LIFE IS COURSE CORRECTING

Once I make my best educated guess as to whether I'm serving ego or love (i.e., my authentic self—to slightly modify Martha Beck's phrasing), [76] I take the action and whatever happens, happens. Looking back, I'll have the results of that experiment, which I can incorporate into my body of knowledge the next time I encounter moments of indecision.

If I made a mistake, I do my best to clean it up and learn from it.

I have a tendency to overcompensate, and let the pendulum swing too far to the opposite side. In the years I was

---

76 Elizabeth Gilbert and Martha Beck, "Episode 208: Leap Into the Fire," September 16, 2016, Magic Lessons with Elizabeth Gilbert, podcast, 1:19:28.

recovering from my workaholic burnout, I noticed myself being extremely rigid about my work-related boundaries. Some of that was due to emotional exhaustion from the trauma therapy work I was also doing at the time. Some of it was out of fear that if I gave an inch, my employer would take a mile, and I'd end up back in the same devastated condition as before.

Life is a gentle teacher. In the same way life showed me when it was time to slow down, life also let me know when it was time to pick up the pace slightly.

THE DECISION THAT MATTERS MOST

The more I work on healing the wounded parts of me that cause my ego to spring into action and begin making noise, the more I'm convinced that there's only one decision that matters.

Since we can only serve love or ego, which one will we choose?

APPENDIX

———

Introduction

- Bauer, Jack J. & Heidi A. Wayment, "The psychology of the quiet ego" in *Decade of Behavior. Transcending Self-Interest: Psychological Explorations of the Quiet Ego.* Eds. H. A. Wayment & J. J. Bauer, 7–19. Washington, D.C.: American Psychological Association, 2008.

- Clifton, Jim. "The World's Broken Workplace." Gallup.com. Accessed on September 28, 2019. https://news.gallup.com/opinion/chairman/212045/world-broken-workplace.aspx?g_source=position1&g_medium=related&g_campaign=tiles

- Clifton, Jim. "What Happiness Today Tells Us About the World Tomorrow." Gallup.com. Accessed on September 27, 2019. https://news.gallup.com/reports/220601/what-happiness-today-tells-us-about-the-world-tomorrow.aspx

- Jung, Carl. Qtd. In "C.G. Jung: Quotable Quotes." Goodreads (website). Accessed December 20, 2019. https://www.goodreads.

com/quotes/634512-intuition-does-not-denote-something-contrary-to-reason-but-something

- Kaufman, Scott Barry. "The Pressing Need for Everyone to Quiet Their Egos." *Scientific American*. May 21, 2018. Accessed on December 21, 2019. https://getpocket.com/explore/item/the-pressing-need-for-everyone-to-quiet-their-egos?utm_source=pocket-newtab

- Mann, Annamarie, and Jim Harter. "The Worldwide Employee Engagement Crisis." Gallup.com. Accessed on September 28, 2019. https://www.gallup.com/workplace/236495/worldwide-employee-engagement-crisis.aspx

- Moyer, MD, Nancy. "Amygdala Hijack: When Emotion Takes Over." Healthline.com. April 22, 2019. Accessed on January 25, 2020. https://www.healthline.com/health/stress/amygdala-hijack#symptoms chapter number

- Wayment, PhD, Heidi A. and Jack J. Bauer, PhD., eds. *Transcending Self-Interest: Psychological Explorations of the Quiet Ego*. Washington D.C.: American Psychological Association, 2008.

Chapter 2: Are You There Stevie? It's Me, Stephanie

- "About." EllenLanger.com (website). Accessed December 26, 2019. http://www.ellenlanger.com/about/

- Colbert, Stephen. Interview by Anderson Cooper. *Anderson Cooper 360 Degrees*. August 15, 2019. Accessed on December

26, 2019. http://transcripts.cnn.com/TRANSCRIPTS/1908/15/
acd.02.html

- Deloria, Jr., Vine. Qtd. In "Vine Deloria, Jr.: Quotable Quotes."
  Goodreads (website). Accessed December 20, 2019. https://
  www.goodreads.com/quotes/160879-religion-is-for-people-
  who-re-afraid-of-going-to-hell

- Jobs, Steve. Stanford Commencement Address. June 14,
  2005. Accessed December 26, 2019. https://news.stanford.
  edu/2005/06/14/jobs-061505/

- Langer, Ph.D., Ellen J. *Mindfulness*. A Merloyd Lawrence Book,
  Da Capo Press, 1989.

- Stuver, Hank. "2019's Best TV moment? It was Stephen Colbert
  Answering Anderson Cooper's Question About Grief." *The
  Washington Post*. December 23, 2019. Accessed on December
  26, 2019. https://www.washingtonpost.com/entertainment/
  tv/2019s-best-tv-moment-it-was-stephen-colbert-answering-
  anderson-coopers-question-about-grief/2019/12/23/ff7cec4e-
  236b-11ea-a153-dce4b94e4249_story.html

Chapter 3: Gold Dust and the "W"

- Bauer, Jack J. & Heidi A. Wayment, "The psychology of the
  quiet ego" in *Decade of Behavior. Transcending Self-Interest:
  Psychological Explorations of the Quiet Ego*. Eds. H. A. Wayment & J. J. Bauer, 7–19. Washington, D.C.: American Psychological Association, 2008.

- Kaufman, Scott Barry. "The Pressing Need for Everyone to Quiet Their Egos." *Scientific American*. May 21, 2018. Accessed on December 21, 2019. https://getpocket.com/explore/item/the-pressing-need-for-everyone-to-quiet-their-egos?utm_source=pocket-newtab

- Tesser, Abraham. "On the Plasticity of Self-Defense." *Current Directions in Psychological Science* 10 no. 2 (April 2001): 66-69.

- Tesser, Abraham & Crepaz, Nicole & Collins, Jon & Cornell, David & Beach, Steven. "Confluence of Self-Esteem Regulation Mechanisms: On Integrating the Self-Zoo." *Personality and Social Psychology Bulletin* 26, no. 12 (November 2000):1476–1489.

- Wayment, Heidi A., Bill Wiist, Bruce M. Sullivan, Meghan Warren, "Doing and Being: Mindfulness, Health, and Quiet Ego Characteristics Among Buddhist Practitioners." *Journal of Happiness Studies* 12, no. 4 (July 2010): 575–589. https://www.researchgate.net/profile/Heidi_Wayment/publication/225470995_Doing_and_Being_Mindfulness_Health_and_Quiet_Ego_Characteristics_Among_Buddhist_Practitioners/links/5c7d9019458515831f83d161/Doing-and-Being-Mindfulness-Health-and-Quiet-Ego-Characteristics-Among-Buddhist-Practitioners.pdf

- Weirsma, Stan., personal communication with Harmon Hook, qtd. in Eleventh Annual Wiersma Memorial Lecture final program, Calvin College Festival of Faith and Writing, 2000.

Chapter 4: Mindfulness Practices: Start Exploring and Keep Evolving

- Anastacio, Barbara. "First Hand: The Rock's Philosophy, As Told Through His Own Two Hands." *The Wall Street Journal.* (Online.) December 3, 2019. Accessed on January 11, 2020. https://www.wsj.com/articles/the-rock-dwayne-johnson-profile-jumani-2-11574273070

- Cameron, Julia. *The Artist's Way: A Spiritual Path to Higher Creativity.* (New York: Penguin Putnam Inc.). 1992.

- Eells, Josh. "The Rock, From Strength to Strength." *The Wall Street Journal.* (Online.) December 3, 2019. Accessed on December 9, 2019. https://www.wsj.com/articles/the-rock-dwayne-johnson-profile-jumani-2-11574273070?mod=rocksocial

- Johnson, Dwayne. "Dwayne 'The Rock' Johnson's Speech Will Leave You Speechless - One of the Most Eye Opening Speeches." MotivationHub. August 7, 2018. Accessed January 3, 2020.

- Johnson, Dwayne. Facebook post. March 19, 2015. https://www.facebook.com/DwayneJohnson/photos/in-hawaii-we-have-a-word-called-mana-which-means-spirit-warrior-mana-is-my-found/10153335708699384/

Chapter 5: In Praise of the Pupa

- The Academy of Natural Sciences of Drexel University. "Butterfly Life Cycle." ANSP.org (website). Accessed on January 4, 2020. https://ansp.org/exhibits/online-exhibits/butterflies/lifecycle/

- Cambell, Joseph. A Joseph Campbell Companion: Reflections on the Art of Living. Eds. Joseph Campbell, Robert Walter, David Kudler. San Anselmo, CA: Joseph Campbell Foundation, 2011.

- Jabr, Ferris. "How Does a Caterpillar Turn into a Butterfly?" *Scientific American*. August 10, 2012. Accessed on January 4, 2020. https://www.scientificamerican.com/article/caterpillar-butterfly-metamorphosis-explainer/

Chapter 6: Your "W" Is Your Work...However You Define it

- Jobs, Steve. Stanford Commencement Address. June 14, 2005. Accessed December 26, 2019. https://news.stanford.edu/2005/06/14/jobs-061505/

- Lamott, Anne. *Bird by Bird: Some Instructions on Writing and Life*. Anchor Books, 1995.

- Sohn, Ian. LinkedIn post. Accessed on July 4, 2019. https://www.linkedin.com/posts/iansohn_i-never-need-to-know-youll-be-back-online-activity-6535470294486839296-sXk4

- Tesser, Abraham & Crepaz, Nicole & Collins, Jon & Cornell, David & Beach, Steven. "Confluence of Self-Esteem Regulation Mechanisms: On Integrating the Self-Zoo." *Personality and Social Psychology Bulletin* 26, no. 12 (November 2000):1476–1489.

Chapter 8: The Juice Is Worth the Squeeze

- Gilbert, Elizabeth and Martha Beck. "Episode 208: Leap Into the Fire." September 16, 2016. Magic Lessons with Elizabeth Gilbert. podcast, 1:19:28. https://maximumfun.org/episodes/magic-lessons-with-elizabeth-gilbert/magic-lessons-ep-208-leap-fire-featuring-martha-beck/

- Holson, Laura. "Reimagining Norman Rockwell's America." *New York Times*, November 8, 2018. Accessed on August 20, 2019. https://www.nytimes.com/2018/11/08/arts/norman-rockwell-freedom.html

- Shedden, David. "Today in Media History: Mr. Dooley: 'The job of the newspaper is to comfort the afflicted and afflict the comfortable.'" Poynter. October 7, 2014. Accessed on August 20, 3019. https://www.poynter.org/reporting-editing/2014/today-in-media-history-mr-dooley-the-job-of-the-newspaper-is-to-comfort-the-afflicted-and-afflict-the-comfortable/

- Totally History (website). "Freedom of Worship." Accessed on January 25, 2020. http://totallyhistory.com/freedom-of-worship/

Chapter 9: Finding the Balance

- Defined Strength and Conditioning (website). "The Coaching Team." Accessed January 23, 2020. https://defined.training/the-coaching-team/

- Goodreads (website). "The Essential Rumi." Accessed October 11, 2019. https://www.goodreads.com/work/quotes/965212-essential-rumi